$20
PEAR:; Theater
ex-lib

Ew 5l12c

WILDEST DREAMS

Born in London in 1939, Alan Ayckbourn spent most of his childhood in Sussex and was educated at Haileybury. Leaving there one Friday at the age of seventeen, he went into the theatre the following Monday and has been working in it ever since as, variously, a stage manager, sound technician, lighting technician, scene painter, prop-maker, actor, writer and director. These talents developed thanks to his mentor, Stephen Joseph, whom he first met in 1958 upon joining the newly formed Library Theatre in Scarborough. He was a BBC Radio Drama Producer from 1965 to 1970, returning to Scarborough to take up the post of Artistic Director of the Theatre in the Round, left vacant after Stephen Joseph's death in 1967. He has premiered over forty of his plays at this Yorkshire theatre where he spends the greater part of the year directing other people's work. Some twenty-nine of his plays have subsequently been produced either in the West End, at the RNT or the RSC. They have been translated into forty languages and have been performed throughout the world, receiving many national and international awards in the process.

by the same author

A CHORUS OF DISAPPROVAL
WOMAN IN MIND (DECEMBER BEE)
A SMALL FAMILY BUSINESS
HENCEFORWARD
MR A'S AMAZING MAZE PLAYS
MAN OF THE MOMENT
INVISIBLE FRIENDS
THE REVENGERS' COMEDIES
TIME OF MY LIFE

WILDEST DREAMS

Alan Ayckbourn

faber and faber
LONDON · BOSTON

First published in 1993
by Faber and Faber Limited
3 Queen Square London WCIN 3AU

Photoset in Plantin by Parker Typesetting Service, Leicester
Printed in England by Clays Ltd, St Ives plc

Alan Ayckbourn is hereby identified as author of this work
in accordance with section 77 of the Copyright, Designs
and Patents Act 1988

All rights whatsoever in this play are strictly reserved
and applications for permission to perform it, etc., must be made
in advance, before rehearsals begin, to Casarotto Ramsay Ltd,
National House, 60–66 Wardour Street, London, WIZ 3HP

A CIP record for this book is available from the
British Library

ISBN 0-571-17304-7

2 4 6 8 10 9 7 5 3 1

CHARACTERS

STANLEY INCHBRIDGE (Alric, The Old Wise One; 48)

HAZEL INCHBRIDGE (Idonia, The Child of Many Tongues; 43)

WARREN WRIGLEY (Xenon, The Stranger; 17)

RICK (ALICE) TOLLER (Herwin, The Battle Companion; 21)

MARCIE BANKS (Novia, The Newcomer; 22)

AUSTEN SKATE (50)

THELMA WRIGLEY (40)

LARRY BANKS (35)

The voices of Pat Toller and Ken Martin

SCENE
The Inchbridges' sitting room, Warren's attic and
Rick's basement

TIME
One December

Wildest Dreams was first performed in Scarborough at the Stephen Joseph Theatre in the Round on 6 May 1991. The cast was as follows:

STANLEY INCHBRIDGE	Barry McCarthy
HAZEL INCHBRIDGE	Anna Keaveney
WARREN WRIGLEY	Gary Whitaker
RICK TOLLER	Isabel Lloyd
MARCIE BANKS	Rebecca Lacey
AUSTEN SKATE	Peter Laird
THELMA WRIGLEY	Elizabeth Rider
LARRY BANKS	Glyn Grain
Director	Alan Ayckbourn
Designer	Roger Glossop
Lighting	Mick Hughes

The play subsequently performed by the Royal Shakespeare Company in The Pit on 14 December 1993. The cast was as follows:

STANLEY INCHBRIDGE	Barry McCarthy
HAZEL INCHBRIDGE	Brenda Blethyn
WARREN WRIGLEY	Gary Whitaker
RICK TOLLER	Jenna Russell
MARCIE BANKS	Sophie Thompson
AUSTEN SKATE	Peter Laird
THELMA WRIGLEY	Andree Evans
LARRY BANKS	Paul Bentall
Director	Alan Ayckbourn
Designer	Roger Glossop
Lighting	Mick Hughes

ACT I

SCENE I

A multiple set.

The main area is taken up with Hazel and Stanley Inchbridge's ground-floor sitting room. Or, more correctly, the sitting room which HAZEL *and* STANLEY *occasionally occupy, since, as he never ceases to remind them, a good half of the room is the property of Hazel's brother,* AUSTEN SKATE.

It is an unexceptional front room in an ordinary, modern semi-detached house in an unremarkable street in an undistinguished town.

The furnishings consist of a two- or three-piece suite, one or two occasional tables and four upright chairs (a couple of them apparently gathered from other parts of the house), grouped round a drop-leaf table which is presently extended and pulled out into the centre of the room.

A 'coal-effect' electric or gas fire. A bright overhead 'chandelier' and one or two table or standard lamps. A sideboard. One door and a bow window.

A slightly smaller area represents the basement in Rick (Alice) Toller's house. This, by contrast, is dirty and untidy – a tip. It was possibly the old kitchen or scullery of the large Victorian terraced house of which it is part. It doesn't look as if it's been properly redecorated since.

There is little light from either the barred subterranean windows or the inadequate overhead naked bulb. A camp bed in the corner. A small table. An easy chair. An upright chair. A small electric fire. Other junk.

Three exits, one via a door, presumably once the tradesman's entrance, leading directly to the outside and the basement-area steps. Another, via a flight of stairs, up to the ground floor of the house. The third, a doorway that apparently links through to the rest of the cellar.

The third playing area is even smaller. This is the attic in a modern estate house. It has been converted into Warren Wrigley's study-bedroom-den.

It consists almost entirely of computers or computer-driven equipment. There is a swivel chair in the midst of it from which WARREN *controls his world. A small bed in the corner. Orderly piles of computer mags and books.* WARREN *is a creature of method and tidiness.*

There is only one entrance to the room, which is via a trap door in the floor. This leads to the first-floor landing of the house, though we see nothing of this. Just the tip of an extending metal ladder which provides access.

At the start only the Inchbridges' sitting room is lit, and that very sparingly, even dramatically, by a clip-on anglepoise lamp fastened to the edge of the main table.

The light is thus cast downwards on to the surface, which is entirely covered by the map of the Game. This consists of a simple light-coloured board subdivided into squares. These are permanently etched on and sealed in, allowing players to draw in crayon over the board to mark out temporary features which can later be erased. Several of these are drawn at present, marking rivers and topographical features in different colours.

There are four model figures occupying four adjacent squares, apparently in the process of crossing the board. Like the board, these are good even if they are home-made. The first of them is the figure of a wise 'ancient', Alric, stooped and elderly, with a stick and flowing robes. The second, Idonia, the mystic and magical one, childlike, beautiful in a dress and with a mane of flowing hair. Next, a strange green-faced creature, half man, half beast – Xenon – the stranger or alien, possessor of special powers of sight and hearing. Finally, the compact, powerful figure of Herwin, the masculine-named female warrior, armoured, carrying a broadsword drawn, shield held ready in case of sudden attack.

The light from the board is reflected upwards into the faces of four people controlling these figures. Moving Alric is STANLEY INCHBRIDGE, *in his forties, of slight build, a schoolteacher with a gentle but sadly often ineffectual disposition. Controlling Idonia is his wife,* HAZEL. *Never a great beauty, time has not treated* HAZEL *kindly. A few years younger than* STANLEY, *she looks every bit her age despite, or perhaps indeed because of, her frenzied attempts to keep middle age at bay.* WARREN WRIGLEY *controls the half-man, half-*

beast Xenon. WARREN *is about seventeen, a pupil of* STANLEY. *A large boy with more than his fair share of spots, he is a boffin and a loner.* WARREN *has no friends of his own age, nor does he any longer seek them, preferring the company of adults such as* STANLEY *and* HAZEL, *with whom he is at ease and outgoing; this couple have become almost surrogate parents to him. All* WARREN *lacks is a girl. But they too avoid him. Especially the fourth member of the group,* RICK (ALICE) TOLLER, *who is represented on the board by Herwin, the warrior.* RICK *is in her early twenties, small and undernourished. She appears to have a permanent cold. She makes little of her appearance and doesn't care. She rarely speaks. She's the introvert of the group. Troubled and private. Yet somehow, thanks to Stanley and Hazel's coaxing and encouragement, she finds her way to their house once a week.*

At present, the group are all gazing intently at the playing board – their concentration absolute. The 'voices' their characters use are not overdone.

HAZEL: (*In a child's voice*) Whither shall we proceed, Alric, O Wise Leader?

STANLEY: (*An older voice*) We must ask that of Xenon, the Far-sighted One. Whither now, Xenon?

WARREN: (*A slight sing-song, 'alien' tone*) I look, Ancient One. With my great non-human sight, I look. To the north are hills, the Mountains of Ag. Beyond that lies the Kingdom of Endocia, the Virgin Queen, Ruler of the Fish People. To the west, the Kingdom of Orrich, Lord of all oak trees and the Forest of Emptiness. To the east, the Grey River, which winds into the Valley of Disappointment and Despair.

STANLEY: And to the south?

WARREN: There lie-eth the Dead Place. The land ruled over by Balaac, the Beast.

HAZEL: (*Breathlessly*) Balaac!

WARREN: With my great hearing I hear him. I hear his footfalls.

HAZEL: Then that's the way we must go!

STANLEY: Ah, yes, but caution, caution. Despite your gifts, you are still a child and impetuous, Idonia. We must prepare and gather our strength. Only then may we hope to attack and win against Balaac, the Beast.

3

WARREN: True. True. The Old One speaks true.

STANLEY: We must prepare ourselves. Are we all agreed?

HAZEL: We are agreed, O Venerable and Wise Leader.

WARREN: You speak wisely, Ancient One.

STANLEY: What say you, Herwin, Silent Battle Warrior?

HAZEL: Herwin? What say you?

RICK: (*Muttering, self-consciously*) Yes, fine. That's OK by me.

HAZEL: (*Prompting, a little impatiently*) O Wise Leader.

RICK: O Wise Leader.

STANLEY: When next we meet, then, it is to the south we travel. What dangers foresee you for us, Idonia, Enchantress and Child of Many Tongues?

HAZEL: (*Using one of her many tongues*) Daire-straidle more-dardle-haire. Alric, Wise One, I see-eth much danger for us all. Even Herwin, the Warrior, needeth all her strength to defeat the might of the Evil Balaac. Yea, even Xenon, the Stranger, needeth all his mighty unworldly powers. Broole-hardle.

WARREN: Xenon will be ready. And so will Herwin, the Fearless. (*To* RICK) Won't you?

RICK: Yeah.

STANLEY: So be it. It is agreed. Then onward!

HAZEL: Onward!

WARREN: Onward!

RICK: Onward!

STANLEY: But now let us pitch camp, for I, the oldest amongst you, would fain rest before our journey.

HAZEL: We will rest with you, O Leader.

STANLEY: (*Less authoritatively*) And also it is now (*Glancing at his watch*) just after twenty to ten, so I think it's probably time to break it up for this evening.

HAZEL: (*Rising*) Heavens! Is that the time?

STANLEY: Yes, I'm afraid that little adventure will have to wait until next Thursday.

(HAZEL *has switched on the overhead light. The room is suddenly very bright.*)

HAZEL: I didn't realize it was that late. He'll be back in a minute demanding his sandwiches.

(STANLEY *starts to unplug and unfasten the anglepoise.* WARREN *puts away the game pieces and folds up the board.* RICK *has gone into the hall.*)

STANLEY: Ah, well, once you're in that other world . . .

HAZEL: (*Drily*) . . . some of us don't want to leave it . . .

STANLEY: Well, I wouldn't say that, I wouldn't say that, Hazel. It's only a bit of fun, you know. That's all.

(HAZEL *goes out, taking one of the chairs which belongs in the kitchen.*)

HAZEL: (*As she goes*) Oh dear, we mustn't get fun muddled up with life, must we? Fatal.

STANLEY: (*Ignoring this*) Thank you very much, Warren. The usual place, would you?

WARREN: Yes, Mr Inchbridge. (*He puts the board and figures, in a box, away in a sideboard drawer.*)

STANLEY: And I think again we have to thank you for another exciting adventure tonight, Warren. Well done.

WARREN: Thank you, Mr Inchbridge.

(RICK *returns, during the next, from the hall, fastening up her motor-cycling gear.*)

STANLEY: That snake monster was quite vivid. Terrifying.

WARREN: Worm. It was a worm.

STANLEY: Worm. Sorry, yes.

WARREN: Tagrath of the Worm People.

STANLEY: Ah, well, we made short work of that. Thanks to Herwin there.

(RICK *manages a brief smile.* HAZEL *returns for the second kitchen chair.* WARREN *starts to go off to the hall to put his coat on.*)
You're off, then, Rick, are you?

RICK: Yes. I've got to get back.

HAZEL: You've got enough to eat at home now, have you? (*Handing* WARREN *the chair*) Take this with you, Warren. (*To* RICK) Have you got food in?

RICK: Yes.

HAZEL: You're eating properly?

RICK: Yes, when I want to.

HAZEL: Whatever that means. We've got half a pie left in the fridge. A steak and kidney pie. I'll wrap that up for you.

5

RICK: No, really . . .

STANLEY: She's all right, Hazel.

HAZEL: None of us are going to eat it, are we? You're not. You just sit there picking out the kidney. And Austen refuses to eat reheated meat. It'll only go to waste.

RICK: I'm fine, really. No problem. 'night.

(WARREN *enters at this point and allows her to pass him in the doorway. He has on his anorak and scarf.*)

WARREN: (*To* RICK) 'night.

STANLEY: Good-night, Rick.

(RICK *escapes and goes.*)

You mustn't crowd the girl, you know, Hazel.

HAZEL: It's stupid. I'll only finish up throwing it away.

STANLEY: She can't balance a great pie dish on her motor-bike, can she? Are you off, Warren?

HAZEL: (*Gathering up the lamp from the table*) I could have wrapped it up for her.

WARREN: Yes, Mr Inchbridge. Thank you.

HAZEL: I'd've put a bag round it for her. Now it's just going to go to waste, isn't it . . .?

(HAZEL *goes out with the anglepoise lamp, speaking as she goes.* STANLEY *has picked up a foolscap envelope from the sideboard.*)

STANLEY: Thank you for this, Warren. I'll certainly have a look at it before next week. It's a short story, you say?

WARREN: It's in the form of a personal statement, Mr Inchbridge. Based on scientifically proved facts.

STANLEY: (*Politely*) Oh, how interesting.

WARREN: It's more than just a short story.

STANLEY: (*Only mildly enthusiastic*) Right. Excellent. Now, you are doing a little bit of exam revision as well I hope, Warren.

WARREN: Oh, yes, Mr Inchbridge . . .

STANLEY: Not just working on these games? And stories? Splendid as they may be.

WARREN: No. I've been revising my notes every day. (*Indicating the envelope*) But I think that could change things, Mr Inchbridge. Change things as we perceive them now.

STANLEY: Yes, I do hope you are revising, Warren, because, as I

6

said, you're not going get there without a good bit of
effort . . .
WARREN: I am. I promise. I am.
(HAZEL *returns and lays a small cloth on the table. She takes a
couple of mats and a cruet from the sideboard during the next.*)
HAZEL: (*Speaking as she enters*) . . . I mean I do, I worry about
that child, I do. She's all alone in that great big house. I
mean, her mother just left her there, didn't she? Just took off
with that – man of hers – with not so much as a postcard –
left the poor kid to fend for herself. I mean, I think that
woman should have been prosecuted, I really do. Her own
daughter . . . (*She goes out again.*)
STANLEY: (*After her, ineffectually*) That was years ago, Hazel, it's
under the bridge . . . What I'm saying is, Warren, if you put
as much effort and ingenuity into your exam results as you
put into these games of yours, you'd end up with a
scholarship to Cambridge.
WARREN: Yes, Mr Inchbridge. I don't want to go to Cambridge,
Mr Inchbridge.
STANLEY: Well, anywhere you chose.
WARREN: I want to stay here.
STANLEY: You've got a good brain, Warren. It's a special brain.
So use it well, lad.
WARREN: I will, Mr Inchbridge.
STANLEY: How's your mother?
WARREN: (*Dully*) She's OK.
STANLEY: Keeping well, is she?
WARREN: Yes. I'll say good-night, then.
STANLEY: Yes, good-night, Warren.
(HAZEL *comes hurrying back with a tray. On the try are some
sandwiches wrapped in clingfilm and a mug of milk similarly
covered. She lays these out on the table.*)
HAZEL: (*Talking as she enters*) . . . I mean, God knows if she eats at
all. I've never seen her eat. Have you ever seen her eat? I
haven't. We've only her word for it she eats at all, haven't
we?
STANLEY: Well, she's a grown woman now, Hazel. And that's all
under the bridge, isn't it?

7

HAZEL: That's where she'll probably finish up . . .

WARREN: Good-night, Mrs Inchbridge.

HAZEL: She's got that permanent cold. Runny nose . . . Good-night, Warren, see you next week.

WARREN: Right.

STANLEY: Well, I'm no longer her teacher. I've no authority over her, have I?

HAZEL: How's your mother, Warren?

WARREN: (*As before*) The same as usual.

STANLEY: I haven't taught her for five years.

HAZEL: Give her my best, won't you?

WARREN: Yes. Good-night, Mr Inchbridge.

STANLEY: Good-night, Warren.

(*As he leaves,* WARREN *nearly collides with* AUSTEN *coming in.* AUSTEN *is about fifty, a thick-set man of great authority. There is little doubt as to who is in real charge in this household. This evening he has had a couple of drinks – just enough to make him merry.*

He still has on his scarf and overcoat, which he now starts to remove.)

WARREN: Sorry, Mr Skate.

AUSTEN: (*Cheerfully*) All finished playing, have we?

WARREN: Good-night. (*He goes.*)

AUSTEN: (*Calling after him*) How's mother?

WARREN: (*Off*) Still there.

STANLEY: I'll see you off, Warren.

AUSTEN: I hope I haven't disturbed the playmates.

HAZEL: Let me take your coat, Austen.

(STANLEY *goes out.* AUSTEN *hands her his coat and scarf during the next.*)

AUSTEN: Still, past their bedtime, I expect.

HAZEL: That boy worries me to death as well . . .

AUSTEN: What did we meet tonight? Dragons? Demons?

HAZEL: Your sandwiches are there for you, Austen.

AUSTEN: Hobgoblins? There must have been hobgoblins.

HAZEL: A boy like that needs a father. Even one that drank himself to death.

AUSTEN: What? No hobgoblins? We're slipping, aren't we? Come

along. Come along, now. Someone's slipping. No
hobgoblins. What about elves, then?

HAZEL: (*With his coat*) I'll hang this up.

AUSTEN: Gnomes? Pixies?

HAZEL: (*As she goes*) Don't eat the clingfilm again, will you. (*She goes out with his coat and scarf.*)

AUSTEN: Fairies? Praties? Banshees? Nymphs? Sprites? Bogeymen? Incubi? No succubi? Ghosts? Dwarves? Imps? Spooks?

(HAZEL *returns.*)

Well, you do disappoint me.

HAZEL: I'll bet he eats all the wrong things as well. His skin's in a shocking state. (*She starts to take the clingfilm off the sandwiches.*)

AUSTEN: What about trolls? Did you meet any trolls?

HAZEL: Do you want tea, Austen?

AUSTEN: Dear me. It all sounds very dull. Hardly worth going, by the sound of it. Leprechauns? No. Kelpies?

HAZEL: Or coffee?

AUSTEN: No. Vampires? Harpies? Lycanthropes?

(STANLEY *has come in and similarly ignores* AUSTEN)

Werewolves?

HAZEL: I presume that means neither. Coffee, Stanley?

STANLEY: No, I'll just take my book upstairs, thanks.

AUSTEN: What's that you're reading, then? *Bumper Book for Boys*, is it? *The Beano Annual*? *The Beezer*? *Wizard and Chips*?

STANLEY: Think I'll have an early night.

HAZEL: You'll probably go straight to sleep as well, won't you? Wish we could all do that . . . (*She goes out again.*)

STANLEY: Right. (*Acknowledging the other man's presence for the first time*) 'night, Austen.

AUSTEN: Hey, Stanley! Hey! Before you go up . . .

STANLEY: What?

AUSTEN: Little question for you . . .

STANLEY: Oh, no, not just now, Austen . . .

AUSTEN: No, no. A brain-teaser. This is right up your street. It arose this evening at the club. A question of semantics, Stanley. I thought straight away, Stanley's the man to ask,

he'll know. I said to them, I said, my brother-in-law's an
English teacher. He'll know. He's an expert.

STANLEY: Can't it wait till the morning, Austen?

AUSTEN: You'll like this, it's a good one. Fugue.

STANLEY: I beg your pardon?

AUSTEN: The word fugue. You've heard of that?

STANLEY: Yes.

AUSTEN: Meaning?

STANLEY: Well – a piece of music that repeats on itself . . . I don't
know the technical term for it . . .

AUSTEN: All right. Good. Fair enough. Now. Pay attention.
What is the other meaning of the word fugue?

STANLEY: Other meaning?

AUSTEN: Yes.

STANLEY: Haven't the faintest idea.

AUSTEN: Oh, come on, Stanley. An English teacher. Come on.
Fugue. Fugue. Surely?

STANLEY: (*Irritably*) I'm saying, I don't know. All right, what
does it mean, then? Presumably you know or you wouldn't
be asking me, would you?

AUSTEN: Yes, I do know as it happens. But there's no point in me
telling you, is there? That's not how you learn, is it, Stanley?
How do we learn? We learn by looking it up for ourselves.
That's surely what you teach your students, isn't it? When
you're not on your hands and knees playing games with
them . . .

STANLEY: Please don't start that, Austen . . .

AUSTEN: Look it up. That's how we learn. That's what gives a
person their idiolect. Are you cognizant with that word,
Stanley? Neither was I at one period in my life, but I looked
it up. Idiolect. A person's own individual way of speaking,
that's what it means. I'll give you that one for free.

STANLEY: Thanks very much. Good-night.

(HAZEL *has returned. She and* STANLEY *talk over* AUSTEN,
who booms on regardless.)

HAZEL: Do you want to take up a hot-water bottle, Stanley? I
think it'll be a bit chilly up there. We didn't put the heating
back up.

STANLEY: No, I won't need one. I may have a read in the bath, I'll see.

HAZEL: Don't take all the water if you do, will you? I think I'll have one myself tonight. It's the only thing that might help me relax . . .

STANLEY: You should take a pill if you're tense . . .

HAZEL: (*Leaving*) I can't take any more. I'm full of pills as it is . . .

STANLEY: (*Following her*) He's prescribed them, Hazel, you might as well take them, mightn't you?

AUSTEN: (*Over this last exchange*) I mean, I'm not a teacher, am I? I don't pretend to be a teacher. I'm just a humble member of Her Majesty's Customs and Excise. A mere VAT inspector. But that doesn't stop me looking up a new word every day. It's not part of my job but I'm interested. Whereas for an English teacher, I'd have thought that would have been rather important. Rather vital. Rather exigent, wouldn't you say? If you know what I mean by exigent. Do you know that word, Stanley?

(STANLEY *goes out, followed by* HAZEL. AUSTEN, *still seated and between bites of sandwich, continues speaking loudly after them.*)

I mean, if I were to ask you to perform complex mental arithmetic, I'd understand your reluctance, Stanley. That's not your line, after all. Not your area. That's my area. And it's a skill that, despite this age of computers and calculators, I feel is important for an alert mind to master. It's another discipline, that's all it is. And a very pleasurable one. If I see a column of figures – say, 9543 plus 362 plus 1837 plus 59 – I can immediately say the total equals – (*Merest pause*) – 11811.

(HAZEL *pops her head round the door.*)

HAZEL: Have you got enough sandwiches there, Austen?

AUSTEN: (*Ignoring her*) 11801, I beg your pardon. I do beg your pardon.

HAZEL: I'll be in the kitchen if you want anything. (*She goes out again.*)

AUSTEN: I mean, that's all I'm saying. Don't mind me.

(*He continues to eat.*

11

The lights go down on him slightly. In the basement area,
RICK *lets herself in via the area door and switches on the light.*

After a moment, AUSTEN *goes off, leaving his empty plate and mug on the table.*

RICK *removes her motor-cycling gear and throws it carelessly in a corner. Her house is silent and empty. Just the dripping of a distant tap. Occasional traffic passes above, the lights flashing briefly through her uncurtained windows.*

RICK *locates a tin-opener and, rummaging in a carrier on the floor, produces a tin (possibly of soup or vegetables), which she opens. She finds a spoon, which she wipes on her shirt, and then, seating herself, silently eats the contents of the tin.*

Upstairs, the sudden sound of a woman's footsteps scurrying across the floor. RICK *glances up briefly, then resumes her meal. Silence.*

The lights fade down on her slightly and come up on Warren's attic area, initially unlit apart from the glow from some of his permanently powered-up technical equipment.

The hatchway opens and Warren's head appears through the hole. He climbs through the hatch. As he does so, we hear his mother's voice from below. Presumably THELMA *is standing at the foot of the loft ladder.*

We see very little of her. Occasionally she ventures up the ladder to her son's eyrie, but only the top of her head will be visible when she does, revealing a woman invariably dressed in black with brightly dyed red hair and with the small eyes and coarse features of a very large person indeed. It is doubtful whether she would even fit through the hatchway.

At this stage, all we will hear of her is her voice.)

THELMA: . . . Warren . . . Is that you, Warren?

WARREN: Yes, Mother, it's me. Who else?

THELMA: Are you going to come down and have a cup of tea?

WARREN: I'm a bit busy just now, Mother.

THELMA: I've just made a cup . . .

WARREN: No, thank you.

THELMA: (*Coaxingly*) Lovely nice cup of tea.

WARREN: No, thanks. I have things to do, Mother . . .

THELMA: Cocoa. Lovely delicious hot cup of cocoa, then.

WARREN: No, thank you, Mother. I've got my revision.

THELMA: I'll make you a cocoa. Lovely hot nice delicious cup of –

(WARREN *closes the hatch before his mother can complete her sentence. He removes his anorak and hangs it up neatly. He sits at his console and switches on the computer screen. He closes his eyes and raises his hands, palms outermost.*)

WARREN: (*In a strange voice*) It cannot be long now. It cannot be much longer, Arnie.

(WARREN *opens his eyes. He stares at the screen, then, after a second, starts to type furiously.*

The lights cross-fade back to RICK, *who is finishing her 'supper'. She sits motionless at the table. The tap continues to drip.*

From upstairs a man's heavy footsteps cross the floor above her head. A door slams somewhere overhead. Another set of footsteps – a woman's this time. Voices raised but muffled. RICK *glances up briefly but doesn't move or react. She merely sits listening.*)

KEN'S VOICE: Where the bloody hell is she? I want to know where she is?

PAT'S VOICE: Why don't you leave the kid alone, Ken? Just leave her alone.

KEN'S VOICE: When I find her she's in trouble, I can tell you that. She's in real trouble this time. I'm not having any kid of mine cheeking me like that . . .

PAT'S VOICE: She's not your kid, is she? She's nothing to do with you, is she . . .?

KEN'S VOICE: I'm living here. She's my responsibility while I'm in this house and she'll bloody well do as she's told, even if I have to thrash the daylights out of her. (*Yelling*) Alice! Alice! Come on, I know you're hiding. Alice! You come here this second and eat your tea, do you hear me? Alice! (*His voice recedes.*)

PAT'S VOICE: (*Following him*) Ken, please! Ken, don't please! Just leave the bloody kid alone, why can't you . . .?

(*Their footsteps move away. Another distant door-slam. Silence.* RICK *continues to sit motionless.*

The lights cross-fade back to the Inchbridges' sitting room. The lights are still on though the room is empty. The distant sound of a water tank refilling. HAZEL *puts her head round the door, sees Austen's empty mug and plate and, coming into the room, clears and tidies the table. She is now in her nightclothes.*)

AUSTEN: (*Off*) Good-night, then. Don't dream of ghosts.

HAZEL: Good-night, Austen dear. Sleep well.

(*She finishes her task, gives a final look around the room, gives a little shiver of unhappiness and switches off the light.*

The light returns to WARREN, *who has paused in his typing to read what he has written. As he does this, there is a discreet knocking on the hatchway in the floor.*)

THELMA: (*Her voice muffled*) Warren . . . Warren. Here's your cocoa . . .

(WARREN *scowls but chooses to ignore her. More insistent knocking.*)

Warren. Warren, dear . . .

WARREN: Hallo?

THELMA: (*Her voice*) It's your cocoa, dear. I've brought you up your cocoa.

WARREN: It's open. Just leave it there. Thank you, Mother.

(*The hatch opens cautiously. Thelma's hand appears with a mug of steaming cocoa.*)

THELMA: Here you are, dear. It's lovely and hot.

WARREN: (*Without taking his eyes from the screen*) Thank you.

THELMA: I'm putting it just here. All right?

WARREN: Thank you.

THELMA: Don't let it get cold, will you?

WARREN: No.

THELMA: Drink it while it's hot.

WARREN: Yes.

THELMA: Don't be too late, will you, dear?

WARREN: No.

THELMA: Don't sit in front of those screens too long, will you?

WARREN: No.

THELMA: You know what happened to Mrs Chambers. Looking at screens for too long.

WARREN: Yes.

THELMA: That's how she lost her baby.

WARREN: (*Through gritted teeth*) I'm not having a baby, am I?

THELMA: Good-night, dear. Don't forget to say your prayers, will you?

WARREN: No. Good-night.

THELMA: God bless you. I'll say a little prayer for you as well, dear.

WARREN: Thank you, Mother.

(*The hatch closes.* WARREN *rises and, crossing to it, bolts it shut angrily. He stands for a moment, then, instead of returning to his console, sits on the bed. After a moment, he lies back and stares at the ceiling.*

Retaining this image, we add to it the Inchbridge house and the sitting room in virtual darkness. HAZEL *comes in from the hall. She stands by the window, gazing out. She is lit by the street lamp outside.*

Add to this scene the basement. RICK *rises and takes off her boots and jeans. She climbs into bed in just her pants and T-shirt and snuggles down under the uncovered duvet like a small child with just her eyes showing. A man's footsteps overhead.*)

KEN'S VOICE: (*Calling, coaxingly*) Alice! Alice! Alice!

(RICK *lies there with the light on.*

Hold all three images, then fade down to just the Inchbridges' sitting room as STANLEY, *in pyjamas and dressing gown, looks round the door and sees* HAZEL.)

STANLEY: Oh, hallo. Coming to bed?

HAZEL: Yes, in a minute.

STANLEY: Wondered where you were.

HAZEL: I was . . . (*She tails away.*)

STANLEY: You all right? (*He moves closer to her.*) Hazel? All right?

HAZEL: Not really, no. If you want to know. No. (*She is crying.*)

STANLEY: Hazel? What is it, old love?

HAZEL: Everything really. Us. (*Attempting a smile.*) Life.

STANLEY: Well, yes. That's always worth a cry, is life. Anything special though? Anything more to cry about than usual, is there?

HAZEL: I just looked at the four of us this evening, playing that game. Pretending to be people we weren't. Could never be, any of us. Not in our wildest dreams. I thought, oh dear, that's sad, isn't it? Just look at us all. Two strange kids with no friends of their own except this daft, batty middle-aged couple.

STANLEY: Well, it's just a bit of fun, isn't it? It's not hurting anybody.

HAZEL: I think Austen's right, sometimes. We all ought to be put away.

STANLEY: No, Austen is never right. That's the only thing I know for certain in this world, Hazel. Austen can never be right. Even when he's right, he's wrong, that I do know. So don't go by him.

HAZEL: But what are we doing, Stanley? We can't play games all our lives, can we? Can we? Tell me. What do we both think we're doing?

STANLEY: We're – I think I'm teaching at Whinnythrop Lane and trying to shed a little light here and there to all those young eager minds – some of them – and I think you're –

HAZEL: I'm – ? What?

STANLEY: You're – well, I think you're working for the building society –

HAZEL: Which I don't enjoy . . .

STANLEY: Which you don't enjoy . . .

HAZEL: Which I hate every minute of . . .

STANLEY: Which you hate every minute of, but you'd never think of leaving, would you?

HAZEL: What if I did? What else is there for me to do?

STANLEY: Well . . .

HAZEL: Stay home and look after you and Austen? More than I do already?

STANLEY: Not – necessarily . . .

HAZEL: Well, what else? What else?

STANLEY: I don't know. Maybe we should . . . Maybe we should try and have more fun. Do things together more. More holidays. Little ones. Needn't be that expensive. I mean, we could take weekend breaks. And go for walks. Things like that. Get the old tent out of the attic, why not? Be a laugh, wouldn't it? Go tenting again. Remember the laughs we had? (STANLEY *chuckles*. HAZEL *sobs loudly*.)
Hazel, come on. Come on, old love. Just tell me what you'd

like most. Tell me what you want, we'll try and arrange it . . .

HAZEL: (*Uncontrollably*) I don't know what I want, do I?

STANLEY: (*Miserably*) I'm sorry you're like this. I hate to see you like this. I'm sorry.

HAZEL: I'm sorry.

STANLEY: No. I'm sorry. I don't quite know what to do for the best, Hazel. I'm sorry.

HAZEL: I'm sorry . . .

(*They stand close together, not touching. Silence.*

WARREN *is now asleep on his bed.*

RICK *lies under her duvet, still wide awake. A sudden loud knocking at her front door upstairs.* RICK *reacts, sits up slightly and listens. The knock is repeated, urgently.* RICK *remains frozen, listening.*)

HAZEL: Don't worry, I'll snap out of it, don't worry. You know I get like this sometimes. Don't worry. Go to bed. I'll be up in a second.

(STANLEY *remains where he is, looking at her.*)

I shouldn't get like this. It's very selfish of me. I shouldn't let it get on top of me like this. I mean, you get depressed, I know you do. But you never burden other people with it, that's the difference. You're considerate. You keep it to yourself.

STANLEY: I'm all right. No bother about me.

HAZEL: You're not all right. Don't say you are. I see you sometimes. I notice.

STANLEY: Me? When?

HAZEL: I've seen you. I've noticed.

STANLEY: What?

HAZEL: Well, with Austen. He upsets you terribly sometimes, I know he does.

STANLEY: Nah! Not any more. He used to.

HAZEL: Why do you let him walk all over you? Why don't you stand up for yourself? He'd soon stop once you did. He's a bully, that's all he is. You should talk back at him sometimes.

STANLEY: I don't want to talk back at him. I don't want to talk to him at all.

HAZEL: He – belittles you. That's what he does. And in front of those kids.

STANLEY: Warren and Rick?

HAZEL: Yes.

STANLEY: They don't care. They've got the measure of Austen. Don't worry about them.

HAZEL: I'm not, I'm worrying about you.

STANLEY: I'm all right. I'm not the one who's standing here crying in the dark, am I?

HAZEL: You know what I'm talking about.

STANLEY: I haven't the faintest.

HAZEL: You know. (*Pause.*) You know.

(*A rattling at Rick's basement door.* RICK *sits up, alarmed.*)

MARCIE: (*Her voice through the door*) Rick? Rick? Are you in there? Rick!

(*More rattling at the door.* RICK *gets out of bed and cautiously moves to the door.*)

RICK: Who is it?

MARCIE: (*Through the door*) Rick? Is that you?

RICK: Who's that?

MARCIE: It's me. Marcie. Please let me in, Rick. Please.

RICK: (*Reluctantly*) Just a minute.

(RICK *opens the door to admit* MARCIE. *She is in her early twenties, attractive in a fresh, 'untouched' sort of way. Her normal manner is to give whoever she is with her total, undivided, eager attention – an attractive quality, especially for the majority, who yearn for such a thing. At present* MARCIE *seems a little breathless and flustered. Or at least as breathless and flustered as she can ever become.*)

MARCIE: Hallo. Can I come in? It's important.

RICK: (*Closing the door after her*) What's wrong?

MARCIE: I'm . . . (*Breathless*) I'm . . . Look, may I use your loo?

RICK: (*Indicating*) Yes, along there.

MARCIE: Would you mind awfully?

RICK: Just along there.

MARCIE: Thanks.

(MARCIE *hurries off further into the basement area.* RICK *stares after her, frowning slightly.*)

HAZEL: We should have had children of our own. That's what we should have done.

STANLEY: Oh, come on. Not this again –

HAZEL: We should.

STANLEY: Hazel, we've talked this –

HAZEL: We could have moved away from here. Got our own place – instead of being lodgers like this.

STANLEY: We're not lodgers. This house is half yours –

HAZEL: Lodgers. You know we are. He never lets us forget it. If Mary had lived she'd never have let us stay. She'd have found a way to get us out. She'd have persuaded Austen to buy us out if necessary.

STANLEY: (*A fraction out of patience*) Well, she's dead and we're here and he's here and we haven't got children and it's too late now and it's half-past twelve and we'd better make the best of it, hadn't we?'

(WARREN *wakes with a jolt. He gets off his bed and creeps to the hatchway, unbolts it carefully and, opening it, looks down below. After a brief glance, he starts to descend, closing the hatch behind him.*

HAZEL: (*After a pause*) No. We should have had children. My mistake. Nothing to do with you. All my fault.

STANLEY: You used to say you didn't want them . . .

HAZEL: That's what I used to say. I know I did. Well, I was wrong, wasn't I? I see now, I was wrong.

STANLEY: (*With a sigh*) Oh, dear. (*He moves away from her and sits.*)

HAZEL: You should have made me, Stanley. You should have made me have them.

STANLEY: (*Wearily*) What are you talking about?

HAZEL: You shouldn't have listened to me. You should have just – taken me by force. Forced me to have them.

STANLEY: Oh, Hazel . . .

HAZEL: You think you can beat her – but you never do. She'll get you eventually. She always does. She knows.

STANLEY: Who are we talking about, now?

HAZEL: Nature. Bloody old Mother Nature. She knows. You think you can outsmart her, but you never can. She gets her revenge in the end.

STANLEY: Hazel, it's quarter to one, old love.

(MARCIE *returns. She has tidied herself and now looks almost pristine again. Her normal appearance.* RICK *stares at her.*)

MARCIE: Oh, that's better. Thank you. I didn't know what I was going to do. I was frantic. I thought, where can I go? Who do I know who can help? And then I thought of you, Rick, I hope you don't mind. I remembered I'd taken your address at work. You remember? When we were all of us going to that concert and then you didn't come? Remember? I hope you didn't mind, Rick. I was just so desperate.
(*Slight pause.*)

RICK: To use my toilet, you mean?

MARCIE: What? Oh, no.

RICK: No?

MARCIE: Well, only incidentally. No. It's Larry.

RICK: Larry?

MARCIE: My husband. He – I left him. Tonight. He started hitting me – punching . . .

RICK: Punching you?

MARCIE: Yes. I've got bruises all up my arms – I'll show you if you don't believe me – I always knew he was violent, Rick. Potentially. I mean, he's been in trouble in the past, but I never thought he'd hit *me*. Not me. He loved me – he said he loved me – but tonight he just – came at me – just wild – trying to hit my face – I don't know what I said – I can't think of anything I could have done to make him like that – I covered my head (*Demonstrating*) like this – that's how he bruised my arms. It was terrifying, Rick, just terrifying. No one's ever – ever hit me before. Ever. I was so frightened. I just ran out of the house – just as I was. Like this.
(*She pauses for breath.* RICK *stares at her.*)
Do you – do you have – anything to drink?

RICK: What, you mean like – whisky?

MARCIE: No. Coffee. Anything.

RICK: Tea.

MARCIE: Lovely.

RICK: Bag.

MARCIE: Naturally.

RICK: No milk.

20

MARCIE: Just a teeny drop.

RICK: No, there isn't any.

MARCIE: Oh, right. Perfect.

(RICK *moves away, leaving* MARCIE *to stare round the room somewhat critically. She sits at the table.*)

HAZEL: (*Who has reached a new low*) I sometimes catch myself staring at myself in that bathroom mirror and I think – what have you done with that body, Hazel? What have you done with it, woman? You've wasted it. That's what you've done. Look at it. Shrivelling and drooping and wasting away – covered in brown spots and warts and wrinkles and what use have you ever made of it? Nothing. It's not even produced children.

STANLEY: (*Muttering*) There are other things, aren't there?

HAZEL: (*Sharply*) What? What did you say?

STANLEY: I said there are other things besides children.

HAZEL: What? What else is there? For a woman? That's what we were designed for. What else use are we?

STANLEY: Oh, come on, Hazel, now you're being stupid.

HAZEL: I should have done what my mother did. That's all she did. All her life. Had children and looked after them all her life. That was the natural thing. And she was happy doing it.

STANLEY: What are you talking about? She was as miserable as hell.

HAZEL: She wasn't.

STANLEY: She was the most miserable woman I've ever met.

HAZEL: Nonsense.

STANLEY: She was, Hazel. I remember her.

HAZEL: Only – only towards the end. Most of her life she wasn't. She was only unhappy at the end.

STANLEY: Yes, because she realized she'd wasted her whole bloody life looking after you and Austen.

HAZEL: At least she had us. What have I got?

STANLEY: (*Muttering*) Me.

HAZEL: What?

STANLEY: I said me. You've got me.

(*Silence.*)

Hazel, it's quarter-past one.

(WARREN *emerges again through his hatchway. He has made himself an enormous white-bread doorstep sandwich, already half eaten. His cheeks are bulging. He closes the hatch and rebolts it. He sits back on the bed and eats.*)

HAZEL: I've wasted this body. I haven't even given pleasure with it.

STANLEY: You did to me . . .

HAZEL: No, I didn't. I just lay there. Like a plank. Rigid. I was terrified of the whole business.

STANLEY: Well, that's various things. Me among them. It was probably me. Most probably, looking back. I don't know.

HAZEL: No. It was my fault. I should have put you at your ease. That's what a woman's meant to do. That's her job.

STANLEY: It's nobody's job. It's not a job, Hazel. Sex isn't a job. It's supposed to be – spontaneous – and effortless – and easy.

HAZEL: If it's that easy, why do they need to write all these books explaining it to people? Tell me that. No, it was me. My mother told me once my father used to play her like a violin every night of her married life . . . That's never happened to us.

STANLEY: (*Muttering*) What did you want me to do? Tuck you under my chin?

HAZEL: (*Sharply*) What?

STANLEY: Nothing.

HAZEL: Don't make jokes about it, Stanley, please. Don't joke about it.

STANLEY: Maybe we should, Hazel. Maybe that's the trouble.

HAZEL: It's not a thing to joke about, is it? Surely? No, I think if you want to know, that's been our trouble half the time. I mean – how can you seriously love someone if they keep laughing?

STANLEY: I have no answer to that, Hazel.

HAZEL: Look at the time, it's twenty to two. What are we doing?

STANLEY: No idea at all.

HAZEL: You all right?

STANLEY: No. If you want to know. Not at all. I'm very depressed.

HAZEL: Oh, don't you start. Just because I do. One of us is enough.

STANLEY: Maybe it's connected, Hazel.

HAZEL: I'll make a bottle. (*She moves to the door.*) Are you staying down? Don't stay down too long, will you?
(*She goes out.* STANLEY *sits gloomily in his chair.*
    RICK *returns with two mugs of black tea, the teabags are still in them.*)
RICK: Here.
MARCIE: Lovely.
RICK: Sorry it took so long. That electric kettle's faulty. You have to hold the switch in while it boils.
MARCIE: Oh dear. You ought to get it mended.
RICK: Yes.
MARCIE: You could always boil water in a saucepan whilst it was being fixed.
RICK: Saucepan?
MARCIE: Yes.
RICK: I don't have any saucepans.
MARCIE: No saucepans?
RICK: No. No point. I don't have a stove.
MARCIE: What do you cook on, then?
RICK: I don't cook.
MARCIE: What do you eat?
RICK: Cold.
MARCIE: All the time?
RICK: Or take-away.
MARCIE: Oh. (*She removes her teabag with difficulty.*) Where shall I – ? With this?
RICK: Anywhere. Doesn't matter.
MARCIE: (*Putting it as tidily as she can on the table*) I'll put it here.
RICK: Fine.
    (HAZEL *puts her head round the sitting-room door. She clutches a hot-water bottle.*)
HAZEL: (*Softly*) Stanley . . .
STANLEY: Mmm?
HAZEL: Come on upstairs now, dear. It's nearly two o'clock.
STANLEY: Coming . . .
    (HAZEL *goes out, after a worried look at her husband. In a moment,* STANLEY *follows.*)

MARCIE: Is this – (*Indicating the room*) Is this – just a temporary
　　arrangement, or do you . . .

RICK: What?

MARCIE: Or do you live here all the time? I mean, I was only
　　asking, don't –

RICK: No, this is – sort of permanent. Home, you know.

MARCIE: Who else lives here, then?

RICK: How do you mean?

MARCIE: In this house? Who lives upstairs?

RICK: Nobody. It's empty.

MARCIE: You mean you have the whole house to yourself?

RICK: Yes.

MARCIE: How lucky. Who owns it, then?

RICK: Me.

MARCIE: What?

RICK: I do.

MARCIE: You own this house? All of it.

RICK: Yes.

MARCIE: Then – excuse my asking, but why do you live down
　　here? In the basement? It's a huge house. You could live up
　　there, couldn't you? Surely?

RICK: No.

MARCIE: Why not?

RICK: (*Slightly tense*) Because I prefer it down here.
　　(*Slight pause.*)

MARCIE: How did you get it?

RICK: What?

MARCIE: The house? How do you come to own it?

RICK: It was – left to me . . .

MARCIE: Who by?

RICK: My mother and – My parents . . .

MARCIE: Are they both dead, then?

RICK: No. They left.

MARCIE: When did they leave?

RICK: (*Vaguely*) Oh. Years ago.

MARCIE: I see. (*She is definitely intrigued.*) I never realized you
　　were . . . Well, of course, you don't get time to talk properly.
　　Not at work. One's too busy . . . serving people and –

24

RICK: Washing up.

MARCIE: Exactly.

(*Upstairs the sound of the front-door knocker. They jump.*)
What's that?

RICK: Front door. Upstairs.

(*More knocking.*)

LARRY: (*His muffled voice*) Marcie! Marcie! Are you in there?
Marcie!

MARCIE: (*Breathlessly*) It's Larry.

RICK: How does he know you're here?

MARCIE: I don't know. He must have – Oh, my God! He mustn't
get in.

(*More knocking.*)

RICK: I'll turn out the light.

(RICK *does so. Darkness, except for light through the windows.*)

MARCIE: (*Whispering*) What if he gets in?

RICK: He can't get in, don't worry.

(*A shadow from outside as someone comes down the area steps.*
MARCIE *has risen and backs to a far corner.*)

MARCIE: (*A stifled scream*) Oh, no . . .

RICK: Sssh!

(*Someone tries the door handle.*)

LARRY:(*His voice outside*) Marcie. I know you're in there
somewhere, Marcie. Don't think you can hide from me
because you can't.

(*Pause.*)

Marcie? I'll only be back, Marcie. I'll find you sooner or
later, so why not come home now, there's a good girl.

(*Pause.*)

Marcie?

(*The figure hovers for a moment, then the shadow recedes as we
hear footsteps going back up the steps.*)

MARCIE: Thank heavens.

RICK: Shh! Make sure he's gone.

(*They wait a second or so.*)

OK. Safe now. Better leave the lights off for a bit, though.

MARCIE: Would you – would you mind if I just lay down for a
second? I feel . . . I feel a bit . . .

RICK: Sure. Use the bed. There. Use my bed.

MARCIE: Thanks. Are you sure – ?

RICK: Fine. Why don't you get some sleep? You look as if you need sleep. It's all right, I've got another bed. Use that one.

MARCIE: Thank you. (*She approaches the bed, examines it rather suspiciously, then decides she has little other choice*) You don't – you don't have a spare nightie, do you? (*Looking at* RICK) No. 'jamas? No?

RICK: Sorry.

MARCIE: Oh, well, doesn't matter. What the hell. All girls together, aren't we?

(*She starts to undress, finally stripping down to her bra and pants.* RICK *watches her intently. As* MARCIE *undresses she's unaware of* RICK.)

Just for a second then, I was so frightened. Terrified, you've no idea. I don't know what he'd have done if he'd got in. He'd probably have tried to kill me or something. Both of us. He has this terrible temper, you can't imagine. He nearly went to prison for attacking a man in a betting shop. That was long before he met me, of course . . . (*Aware of Rick's gaze*) What's the matter?

RICK: (*Looking away from her*) Nothing.

(*During the next,* MARCIE *folds up her outer garments neatly on the chair and finally climbs into bed and snuggles under the duvet.*)

MARCIE: He might have killed me, the mood he was in tonight.

RICK: He'd've had to deal with me first.

MARCIE: Well. Possibly. But he's very powerful – I'm going to be an absolute slug tonight, I'm not even going to wash – he used to pick me up sometimes as if I were two stone. He's incredibly strong.

RICK: So am I.

MARCIE: (*Slightly doubtful*) Really? But not –

RICK: And I'm trained.

MARCIE: Trained?

RICK: Unarmed combat. Don't worry. I can take care of myself.

MARCIE: Does it work?

RICK: What?

MARCIE: Unarmed combat?

RICK: Of course it works.

MARCIE: Oh. I sometimes wondered. You hear these stories –

RICK: I could bring a fourteen-stone man to his knees with a broken nose in three and a half seconds.

MARCIE: (*Sleepily*) Golly. That'd teach him.

RICK: I could break his marriage vows with the toe of my boot. Don't worry. You're safe here.

MARCIE: (*Impressed*) That's nice to hear, anyway. (*Suddenly drowsy*) At least I'm in good . . . (*yawning*) . . . At least I'm in good . . . (*Yawning*) . . . sorry . . . hands . . .

(RICK *stands looking at the sleeping figure. Then she gently brushes Marcie's hair from her eyes, adjusts the duvet more snugly around her and finally, spreading out her anorak, curls up at the foot of the bed like a protective dog.*
The lights fade on all areas.)

SCENE 2

The same. A week later. Both Warren's attic and Rick's basement are empty and unlit. The lights are on at the Inchbridges', though. HAZEL *hurries in, wearing an apron, her fist full of cutlery. She looks rather distraught.* STANLEY *follows anxiously, carrying the anglepoise lamp.*

HAZEL: (*Speaking as she enters*) . . . I mean, I've barely finished feeding you and Austen and then we've got those two arriving . . .

STANLEY: It's all right, old love, there's no hurry. No hurry.

HAZEL: (*Replacing the cutlery in the sideboard drawer*) . . . I mean, I wouldn't mind a little time to myself, I really wouldn't. Just occasionally . . .

STANLEY: Well, all right, we'll try and arrange that, then. We'll see what we can arrange . . .

HAZEL: I mean, no wonder I look about a hundred and ten . . . (*She goes.*)

STANLEY: (*Feebly*) You look – fine . . .

(*But* HAZEL *has gone.* STANLEY *sighs and starts to clamp the anglepoise to the table. The doorbell rings.*)

HAZEL: (*A cry from the kitchen*) Oh, no . . .

27

STANLEY: (*Hastily*) It's all right, I'll go, old love, I'll go.

    (STANLEY *hurries out. We hear him admitting* WARREN.)

WARREN: (*Off*) 'evening, Mr Inchbridge.

STANLEY: (*Off*) Good-evening, Warren. Come in, come in.

    (STANLEY *ushers* WARREN *into the room.*)

    Shan't be a moment, we're just a little –

WARREN: (*Glancing round*) Not too early, am I?

STANLEY: No, no. Well, maybe a fraction. Not to worry,
    Warren. Let me take your coat.

WARREN: Thank you, Mr Inchbridge. Only I wondered if we'd
    be able to get a quiet word about 'I, an Alien'.

STANLEY: (*Going out momentarily to hang up Warren's anorak*) I
    beg your pardon?

WARREN: About my statement, 'I, an Alien'. Did you read it?

STANLEY: (*Returning*) Oh yes. Yes, I did. It's – fascinating,
    Warren. Very imaginative. Extraordinary.

WARREN: It's all based on scientific fact.

STANLEY: Well – scientific conjecture, I think would be nearer
    the mark, Warren. I mean to say, we don't have concrete
    proof that there are aliens actually living among us. Not at
    this present time. Of course, it could be that you're right and
    they're here, there and everywhere even as we speak –

WARREN: I am right, Mr Inchbridge.

STANLEY: Possibly. All I'm saying is that we have no proof,
    though, do we?

WARREN: I do, Mr Inchbridge.

STANLEY: Now, that's not technically correct, is it?

WARREN: I'm proof. I am an alien, Mr Inchbridge.

STANLEY: No, now . . .

WARREN: What more proof do you want? It's all here.

STANLEY: No. I think what you're experiencing, Warren, is what
    they call alienation. Which is not altogether uncommon,
    especially at your age, but it's still very different from being
    an alien.

WARREN: Yes, but the word alienation – where does that come
    from in the first place, Mr Inchbridge?

STANLEY: Well, presumably, yes, from the word alien. Granted.

WARREN: Exactly. Now, according to Arnie Van der Hooch . . .

STANLEY: Who?

WARREN: (*Excitedly*) The man whose book I've based that on, we are not one race at all. There is no such thing as mankind as such, Mr Inchbridge. We are, in fact, formed from seven or maybe even eight different inter-galactic species, part of an exploratory expedition that crash-landed here half a million years ago and caused the Grand Canyon.

STANLEY: Now, Warren, that is just conjecture . . .

WARREN: It isn't, not at all. Why do you think people are different colours?

STANLEY: Now, there are reasons for that. This is nonsense.

WARREN: (*Triumphantly*) Then why do you think women are so different from men, Mr Inchbridge? Answer me that?

(*A pause.* STANLEY *is stumped for a reply.*)

STANLEY: (*Gently*) Have you – have you talked to your mother about this, Warren?

WARREN: (*Sulkily*) How can I talk to her? She's an Orgue.

STANLEY: An Orgue?

WARREN: They're a lower life-form. They only brought them along as labour. For menial duties.

(*The doorbell rings.*)

STANLEY: (*Worriedly*) Excuse me, Warren, I'll be back in a minute. Just a moment.

(STANLEY *goes out.* WARREN *stands unhappily.*)

WARREN: He was right. Nobody ever believes it.

(*The sound of* STANLEY *admitting* RICK *and* MARCIE.)

RICK: Evening, Mr Inchbridge . . .

STANLEY: (*Off*) Hallo, Rick, come in . . . Oh, who have we here?

MARCIE: (*Off*) Good-evening, Mr Inchbridge, I'm Marcie Banks. I'm a friend of Rick's, I hope you don't mind . . .

STANLEY: (*Off, uncertainly*) No, no. Not at all. Come in, please.

MARCIE: (*Off*) Thank you.

(*A second later and* STANLEY *ushers in* MARCIE *and* RICK. *They are both clad in motor-cycle kit and carrying their helmets.*)

STANLEY: Do come in. Please come through. This is Warren Wrigley, a pupil of mine . . .

MARCIE: (*Beaming at* WARREN) Hallo, Warren . . .

STANLEY: This is – er – I've forgotten your name again . . .

MARCIE: Marcie. Marcie Banks.

WARREN: (*Gaping at her, totally smitten*) Ur.

STANLEY: Marcie's a friend of Rick's, Warren.

MARCIE: We work together.

STANLEY: Oh, do you? At the –

MARCIE: At the Potty Shrimp. We call it that, anyway. I'm a
waitress.

STANLEY: Oh. How interesting.

(*A silence.*)

MARCIE: Isn't this lovely? What a lovely room.

STANLEY: Yes. Thank you. Let me take your – things . . .

MARCIE: (*Beaming at him*) Thank you, Mr Inchbridge.

STANLEY: (*Rapidly succumbing to her charms as well*) Stanley –
Stanley, if you'd prefer . . .

MARCIE: Right. Thank you.

(*Stanley takes Rick's and Marcie's gear from them. As he is
doing this, there is a crash of breaking crockery from the kitchen
and an accompanying wail from* HAZEL. STANLEY *reacts.*)

STANLEY: Just a moment, please, I'll see what the problem is.
Talk among yourselves. Perhaps you'd like to lay things out,
Warren.

WARREN: (*Who hasn't taken his eyes off* MARCIE) Right, Mr
Inchbridge.

(STANLEY *goes out.*)

MARCIE: (*Turning her attention to* WARREN, *brightly*) Rick tells me
you're a computer wizard, is that right, Warren?

WARREN: (*Muttering, embarrassed*) I know a bit about them.

(*During the next,* WARREN *gets the Game board and pieces from
the sideboard and sets them out.* MARCIE *watches him,* RICK
stands awkwardly by.)

MARCIE: I wish I did. I took a course once but I couldn't come to
terms with them at all. They frighten me to death. They just
sit there whirring at you. I'm terrified I'll press the wrong
button and they'll blow up. Crash or whatever they do.

WARREN: (*Muttering inaudibly*) It's difficult to blow them up.

MARCIE: Sorry?

WARREN: (*A fraction louder*) They're very difficult to blow up.

MARCIE: So they say. You don't know me.

(WARREN *has started to set out the board.*)
Ah! This must be the famous Game?

WARREN: Yes.

MARCIE: Which you invented?

WARREN: Yes.

MARCIE: Hey, genius!

WARREN: (*Warming a little*) Well, in a way. It's based on a standard role-playing game which I update and up-program every week, thus allowing the computer to select and print out variable parameters and random options as and when we require them.

MARCIE: (*Flatly*) No, I don't understand a single word of that. Rick tells me you play every week?

WARREN: Yes.

MARCIE: How nice. And these are all your little people?

WARREN: Yes.

MARCIE: Which one's you?

WARREN: (*Pointing to Xenon*) That one.

MARCIE: Eeek! Terrifying, what is it?

WARREN: That's Xenon. He's the alien. He's from the planet Lakkos.

MARCIE: Wouldn't like to meet him on a dark night.

WARREN: (*Warming up further*) Oh, no. The Laks are known to be extremely friendly and gentle. On Lakkos they're highly civilized. They have advanced sight and hearing. They can hear music from the Milky Way.

MARCIE: I love his face. Why did you choose him?

WARREN: (*Evasively*) I – just did.

MARCIE: (*Smiling at him*) That's fascinating. I'd love to know why.

RICK: (*Suddenly, breaking this up*) That's me, there. Herwin. The Warrior.

MARCIE: (*Picking up Idonia*) This one? Oh, she's beautiful.

RICK: (*Irritably*) No, not that one. That's Idonia – that's Hazel – Mrs Inchbridge. This one. That's Herwin. That's me.

MARCIE: Wow! Now you're talking. Tough.

RICK: Kills anything in her path. Half woman, half machine.

MARCIE: Golly. Idonia's a terribly pretty little girl, though, isn't she? (*Picking up the fourth figure*) And this one must be . . .

31

WARREN: Mr Inchbridge. Alric, the Wise One.

(*As* WARREN *speaks,* STANLEY *re-enters with a couple of kitchen chairs*).

STANLEY: Sorry. Hazel's just coming. Ah, good, you've set it out. Splendid. Explaining it to Marcie? Now, Marcie, would you like to sit and watch or would you like to join in?

MARCIE: Well . . .

RICK: She only came to watch.

WARREN: She can play if she wants to . . .

MARCIE: Would that be all right?

STANLEY: Yes, of course it will. Warren, fetch another chair, would you?

WARREN: Yes, Mr Inchbridge.

(WARREN *heads for the door.* HAZEL *enters at the same moment.*)

RICK: (*To* MARCIE) I thought you only wanted to watch?

MARCIE: Well, it looks such fun.

HAZEL: What's going on? Where are you going, Warren?

WARREN: Fetching another chair, Mrs Inchbridge.

HAZEL: We've got enough, surely?

(WARREN *goes out.*)

STANLEY: Marcie's going to join the game, Hazel. Hazel, this is Marcie. Marcie, my wife, Hazel.

MARCIE: How do you do, Mrs Inchbridge.

HAZEL: (*Distracted*) How do you do. (*Then, ignoring her, to* STANLEY) I don't see how she can, we're half-way through a game.

STANLEY: Well, Marcie can be a character we've met on the way. We're always meeting people on the way.

HAZEL: Yes, but they don't all join us . . .

STANLEY: No, but this one could have done . . .

HAZEL: They don't all tag along, willy-nilly, do they? I mean, if they all joined us there'd be hundreds of them. Innkeepers and hunchbacks and God-knows-what . . .

STANLEY: Yes, but in this case . . .

HAZEL: Woodcutters . . . distressed damsels . . .

(WARREN *re-enters with another chair during the next.*)

STANLEY: Yes, but they didn't have anyone to control them. To play them. Now, there's Marcie . . .

MARCIE: Look, I can just as easily sit and watch if it's a problem . . .

STANLEY: It's no problem. Is it, Warren?

WARREN: No problem.

STANLEY: Rick?

RICK: (*Rather sourly*) Do what you like.

HAZEL: She hasn't even got a piece. She's going to need a piece, a figurine.

STANLEY: We can give her something temporarily. Just for this week. Anything will do. I know, give her a bit of the cruet, that will do for now.

HAZEL: (*Getting the cruet set from the sideboard*) I still think it's very odd indeed.

STANLEY: We can get her something more suitable for next week – assuming she'll be back next week. Can we hope to see Marcie with you regularly, Rick . . .?

RICK: – er . . .

MARCIE: (*Smiling at* RICK) I hope so.

RICK: Yes.

HAZEL: Have you a preference for salt or pepper, Marcie?

MARCIE: Whichever's most convenient, Mrs Inchbridge.

HAZEL: Salt, then.

STANLEY: Now, we must work you out a character, Marcie. Warren? That's usually Warren's department. He's the brains behind the game.

WARREN: She can be Novia. The Newcomer.

MARCIE: (*Savouring the name*) Novia . . .

STANLEY: That suit you, Marcie?

MARCIE: That's a lovely name, thank you.

STANLEY: Right. Down with the lights. On with the game. (STANLEY *switches off the overheads. The board is now illuminated by just the anglepoise as before. He joins them at the table.*)

HAZEL: I don't think I can play for too long tonight. I've got so much to catch up with . . .

STANLEY: Well, you just say when, Hazel. Now, do we have tonight's game parameters, Warren?

WARREN: (*Fishing some computer print-out sheets from his pocket*) Got them here, Mr Inchbridge . . .

STANLEY: Remind us where we were, will you? Get Xenon to remind us. (*To* MARCIE) We always have a little recap at the start, Marcie, just to remind ourselves . . .

MARCIE: Yes . . .

WARREN: To the north are the Mountains of Ag and beyond that the Kingdom of Endocia, the Virgin Queen . . .

MARCIE: Oh . . .

WARREN: . . . Ruler of the Fish People. To the west, the Kingdom of Orrich, Lord of all oak trees and the Forest of Emptiness.

MARCIE: Golly.

WARREN: To the east, the Grey River, which winds into the Valley of Disappointment and Despair.

MARCIE: Aah.

WARREN: And to the south there lie-eth the Dead Place. The land ruled over by Baalac, the Beast.

MARCIE: Wow!

STANLEY: Ah, yes. Of course. We had sighted the Kingdom of Balaac. He whom we had sought for so long, Balaac, the Evil One. Whom we had sworn, each of us for our own secret reason, to destroy. Balaac, the Beast, the reason for our banding together . . .

HAZEL: Yes, we know this, Stanley . . .

WARREN: Alric . . .

HAZEL: We know this, Alric, O Wise One . . .

STANLEY: I speak for the benefit of the fair Novia, the newest amongst us . . . Welcome, child . . .

MARCIE: Hallo, everyone . . .

HAZEL: (*Muttering at her*) Greetings. You're supposed to say greetings . . .

MARCIE: Greetings, everybody . . .

WARREN: We try and talk in old English . . .

STANLEY: Sort of old English. Not genuine, of course. We'd never understand each other at all. But it helps to give it a bit of an atmosphere . . .

MARCIE: Oh, yes. Yea.

STANLEY: So, friends, you have heard from Xenon, the Stranger. We must decide if we are yet strong enough to face the final challenge of Balaac, the Evil One. He whom we have sought these many years . . . What say you, Idonia, Enchantress and Child of Many Tongues?

HAZEL: Strooch-snairt-hooooom-whereno-traaays . . .

MARCIE: (*Whispering*) What did she say?

WARREN: (*Sotto*) She's speaking in one of her many tongues.

HAZEL: Hoore-haaar. I say we should rest further before proceeding, O Wise One. The dangers are many and I see much travail.

STANLEY: Despite your youth, you speak wisely. Xenon?

WARREN: I, too, would advise caution, Alric. The hour is not yet ready. We should travel first to other lands to gain more wisdom and strength.

STANLEY: So be it. What say you, Herwin, the Silent One.

RICK: (*Who's more self-conscious than ever with* MARCIE *there, muttering*) We should wait, O Wise One.

STANLEY: (*Not hearing her*) What sayest thou, Herwin?

RICK: (*Louder*) I say, we should wait, Wise One.

STANLEY: So be it. Then it is the decision of Alric, your leader, that we should travel to the east and the –

MARCIE: I don't think we should. I think we should go after old what's-his-name – Balaac, that's what I think.
(*Silence.*)
Thinketh.

HAZEL: Be silent, Novia. It is not right to question the wisdom of Alric, our leader.

STANLEY: Nay, let the child have speech. What sayest thou, Novia, newest amongst us?

MARCIE: I think we should goeth after this Balaac now. While he's there. I mean, we're a pretty formidable collection, or so it seemeth to me. We haveth Herwin here, who is mighty and strong. And the mega-frightening-looking Xenon with all his powers. And the beautiful enchantress – Mrs . . . sorry . . .

HAZEL: Idonia.

MARCIE: . . . who is obviously bursting with magic. And then there's you, O Wise One. And me. What waiteth we for?
(*A stunned silence.*)

35

STANLEY: Well . . .

HAZEL: (*Muttering*) It is not right that she question your decision, O Leader. She should be punished.

STANLEY: Yes, well, no. Let's consider her point . . .

HAZEL: Your decision is final, O Leader. Thus is it writ.

STANLEY: (*Dithering*) Well, yes, only . . .

WARREN: Maybe she should be heard, O Leader. Maybe we should travel south . . .

HAZEL: We can't travel south. You heard what Alric said –

WARREN: Nay, but she is young and beautiful and of a clear mind . . .

HAZEL: Well, I'm sorry, I'm also young and beautiful and I have to say I think she's wrong . . .

STANLEY: Nay, nay . . .

HAZEL: And she's only just joined us and she should keep her mouth shut . . .

STANLEY: Nay, Idonia child, this is not the way . . .

(*They all start to speak together.*)

RICK: I think we should go east, we're not ready to fight yet. She's only just joined us . . .

WARREN: (*With her*) No, I think she has a point. We should go south and risk it . . .

STANLEY: (*Over them*) Now, now, now, now, now now . . .

MARCIE: (*With them*) Look, I really don't want to cause any trouble. I was only just putting in my suggestion . . .

HAZEL: (*With them*) She's made her suggestion and that's the end of it. Now we do what we decided to do in the first place . . .

STANLEY: (*Shouting them down*) Now wait, wait, wait! PLEASE!

(*Silence.*)

Alric speaks to you. Your leader speaks. If we quarrel amongst ourselves, we will surely perish. Therefore I will choose for us. And I have chosen. We will do as Novia, the Newcomer, suggests and travel south to meet Balaac.

HAZEL: Oh, that's ridiculous.

STANLEY: (*Firmly*) Alric has spoken, child. The Old Wise One has chosen.

HAZEL: (*Under her breath*) Oh, well, if we're going to start taking orders from a salt-cellar . . .

STANLEY: (*Ignoring this*) We are agreed, then, friends? Southwards to the Dead Place, ruled by Balaac himself?

WARREN: Balaac!

MARCIE: Balaac!

HAZEL: (*Rather more reluctantly*) Balaac!

RICK: (*Likewise*) Balaac!

(*At this moment,* AUSTEN *enters, switching on the lights as he does so. He stops as he sees the others sitting there, blinking in the sudden brightness.*)

AUSTEN: Oh, it's you lot. I forgot about you.

HAZEL: Austen, why aren't you at your meeting?

AUSTEN: It was cancelled. Guest speaker taken ill at the last moment . . . I hope you don't expect me to sit in the kitchen while you chase goblins . . .?

HAZEL: (*Rising*) No, no . . .

STANLEY: (*Also rising*) No, we'll – we'll pack in a bit early tonight, I think. We're all a bit tired.

HAZEL: (*Removing the salt-cellar and replacing it in the sideboard*). Yes, I've got masses to get on with . . .

MARCIE: Oh, what a shame.

AUSTEN: Hallo. What's this? A new recruit for the funny farm?

STANLEY: This is a friend of Rick's. Marcie, this is my brother-in-law, Austen, Marcie.

MARCIE: How do you do.

AUSTEN: (*Looking at her approvingly*) Well, well, well . . .

HAZEL: I'll make your sandwiches, Austen. I haven't done them yet. Excuse me.

(HAZEL *goes out.* STANLEY *and* WARREN *start to pack up the game.* RICK *follows* HAZEL *immediately into the hall.*)

AUSTEN: A friend of Rick's?

MARCIE: Yes, we work together, Mr –

AUSTEN: Skate. Austen Skate. Quite presentable, isn't she? Whatever next?

(AUSTEN *laughs.* MARCIE *smiles, embarrassed.*)

How come you know Rick?

MARCIE: Well, we work together, Rick and me.

AUSTEN: Rick and I, not Rick and me. Rick and I, young lady. There's an English teacher in the room, didn't you know? We must mind our Ps and Qs.

RICK: Yes, I'd . . .

AUSTEN: Stanley's usually very strict about things like that. He can't have been listening. Thank your lucky stars, young lady. You might have got six of the best.

(AUSTEN *laughs*. MARCIE *smiles uncertainly*. STANLEY *looks rather apologetic*. RICK *reappears in her motor-cycle gear, carrying her helmet and Marcie's*.)

RICK: You coming, then?

MARCIE: Oh, all right.

STANLEY: No, don't dash away. Stay for a while.

MARCIE: (*Torn*) Well . . .

RICK: No, we have to be off. I need to get back.

MARCIE: Why?

RICK: I need to be going.

MARCIE: We could stay for a little bit, couldn't we?

STANLEY: Please.

RICK: Well, you can if you like. I have to go.

MARCIE: Well, all right . . .

RICK: You coming, then?

MARCIE: No, you go. I'll see you later.

(*Slight pause*.)

RICK: (*Uncertain*) Right. You'll have to walk.

MARCIE: That's OK. Can you take my helmet?

RICK: 'night.

WARREN: 'night

STANLEY: 'night

AUSTEN: Good-night.

(RICK *leaves*.)

STANLEY: Something wrong?

MARCIE: Sorry?

STANLEY: With Rick. She seems a bit – put out.

MARCIE: Really?

(WARREN *has finished packing things away*.)

WARREN: I'll be off too, Mr Inchbridge.

STANLEY: You can't stay either, Warren?

WARREN: No, I need to . . . I have to . . . Good-night, Mr Skate.

AUSTEN: (*In his paper*) Good-night, Warren. Don't get run over by a spaceship, will you?

WARREN: (*Laughing hollowly*) Ha! Ha! Ha! Ha! Ha! I'll try not to, Mr Skate. Good-night – er . . .

MARCIE: Good-night, Warren. (*Smiling*) It's a really great game. See you again soon, I hope.

WARREN: (*Confused*) Yes. Probably.

(WARREN *goes out.* AUSTEN *reads the paper.* STANLEY *smiles at* MARCIE. MARCIE *smiles at* STANLEY. *A silence.*)

MARCIE: Sorry. It's just me, then. Do you want me to go?

STANLEY: No, no. After all, we ought to get to know you a bit, oughtn't we? I mean, you'd hardly walked through the door and you were dragooned straight into our game . . .

MARCIE: Not really. I enjoyed it.

STANLEY: We normally play for hours but . . .

(*They are both very conscious of* AUSTEN, *even though he's pointedly ignoring them.* MARCIE *smiles at* STANLEY. *He smiles at her.*)

AUSTEN: Don't mind me. Don't mind me.

STANLEY: Would you like a cup of tea? Or something.

MARCIE: Thank you.

(HAZEL *hurries in to lay the table, as before.*)

HAZEL: Well, have they all – ? (*She stops as she sees* MARCIE.) Oh, still here?

MARCIE: Yes.

HAZEL: Not gone with Rick?

MARCIE: No.

HAZEL: Oh. Well. Excuse me. (*She carries on with her tasks.*)

STANLEY: We thought we might have a cup of tea.

HAZEL: We? Who's we?

STANLEY: Well, all of us.

HAZEL: All of us?

STANLEY: Yes.

HAZEL: I don't want a cup of tea, I haven't got time.

STANLEY: Ah.

HAZEL: Do you want a cup of tea, Austen?

AUSTEN: No, I don't want a cup of tea.

HAZEL: Right. It's just the two of you, then. Fine. Why didn't you say so in the first place?

STANLEY: I can do it.

HAZEL: (*Going out*) It's no problem at all. (*She leaves.*)

STANLEY: She's – sometimes, my wife's a little . . .

MARCIE: It's all right. I understand. She's like my mother gets . . .

STANLEY: Ah. You live with your parents?

MARCIE: No. I ran away.

STANLEY: Oh.

MARCIE: To get married.

STANLEY: Ah. You're married.

MARCIE: Separated.

STANLEY: Oh.

MARCIE: Yes.

STANLEY: You've obviously crammed quite a lot into a short life.

MARCIE: Yes.

AUSTEN: (*In his paper*) Thirteen shopping days to Christmas. (*He looks up.*) Don't mind me. Don't mind me.
(*Silence.*)

STANLEY: Oh, Lord. Look. He's left his . . . (*He picks up Warren's envelope.*) He's left his short story. Warren. He meant to take it.

MARCIE: I could drop it round to him sometime, if you like.

STANLEY: No, there's no problem. It can always wait till next week.

MARCIE: Please, I'll do it with pleasure. If you have his address.

STANLEY: Yes, I'll let you have it before you –
(*A crash from the kitchen and a cry of irritation from* HAZEL.)

AUSTEN: Dear, dear, dear . . .

STANLEY: Perhaps we'd better . . . Look, would you mind having that tea in the kitchen . . .?

MARCIE: No, not at all. I'd love to see your kitchen, too.

STANLEY: It's nothing very special . . .

MARCIE: I love kitchens.

AUSTEN: Oh, Stanley . . .

STANLEY: Yes?

AUSTEN: Did you ever look up that word I told you about?

40

STANLEY: Word?

AUSTEN: Fugue. Fugue, Stanley. Remember I said it had another meaning?

STANLEY: No, I didn't. Haven't had time.

AUSTEN: Well, I'll tell you. Since you are apparently an English teacher with a reluctance for some reason to consult a dictionary. Fugue can also mean a form of amnesia which is a flight from reality. Isn't that interesting?

STANLEY: Very.

AUSTEN: There you are, young lady, come to this house you can learn something new every day, can't you?

MARCIE: (*Smiling sweetly*) You certainly can, Mr Skate, thank you.

AUSTEN: Don't mind me. Carry on.

(*She and* STANLEY *go out.*

The outside street lights come up on Rick's basement area as she comes in through her door, closes it and, during the next, having laid down her cycle helmets, removes her jacket. She goes off further into the basement for a moment.

AUSTEN *reads the paper.* HAZEL *comes in with his sandwiches.*)

HAZEL: (*Putting the plate on the table*) There you are. (*She sits in the other chair.*) I'll get you your cocoa later. It's still very early.

AUSTEN: (*Sitting*) What are you doing?

HAZEL: What?

AUSTEN: Sitting there? Why are you sitting down?

HAZEL: Why shouldn't I? Do you mind me sitting down?

AUSTEN: You never sit down.

HAZEL: Well, I feel a little in the way in there. Thought I'd better leave them to it.

AUSTEN: Leave them to what?

HAZEL: Oh, nothing. Nothing at all. Nothing.

(AUSTEN *looks at her, then starts reading again, ignoring his sandwiches. Silence for a moment.*)

AUSTEN: Thirteen more shopping days to Christmas.

(RICK *comes back, now dressed for bed – i.e. barefoot in pants and T-shirt. She lies on the bed under the duvet.*

Lights up on Warren's attic as the hatchway opens and
WARREN *emerges. He closes the hatch, bolts it.*

A peal of laughter from MARCIE *in the hall.* STANLEY *puts his head round the door, still smiling.*)

STANLEY: Hazel . . .

HAZEL: Yes?

STANLEY: Marcie's off now, love. She's just off.

HAZEL: (*Not moving*) Oh, right.

(MARCIE *sticks her head round the door.*)

MARCIE: Good-night, Mrs Inchbridge.

HAZEL: Good-night, Marcie.

MARCIE: Thank you for the tea.

HAZEL: My pleasure.

MARCIE: Good-night, Mr Skate.

AUSTEN: Good-night, Marcie.

(MARCIE *goes.*

HAZEL *starts to eat Austen's sandwiches.*

RICK *is still lying on the bed, staring.*)

PAT'S VOICE: (*Calling gently from the top of the stairs*) Alice! Alice! Come on, I know you're down there. Come on up now. He's gone out. Come on. Alice, don't be silly. Alice, he loves you really . . .

(RICK *does not react.*)

At the Inchbridges' STANLEY *returns to sitting room.*

STANLEY: What a nice kid that is.

HAZEL: (*Munching*) Yes?

STANLEY: You should have stayed and talked to her, Hazel. She's a really nice, friendly girl.

HAZEL: Yes.

STANLEY: (*Taking a sandwich as well*) Interested. In other people. That's quite rare these days. So many of them at that age, only interested in themselves. Sad.

HAZEL: Oh, yes.

STANLEY: I think you'd take to her, Hazel, if you gave her a chance.

HAZEL: (*Rising suddenly*) I don't care what you do, Stanley, so long as you get it out of your system. And don't come crying to me when she's had enough of you, that's all.

(*She sweeps out.* STANLEY *sits stunned. He is aware of* AUSTEN.)

42

AUSTEN: (*Smiling*) Don't mind me. Don't mind me.
(STANLEY *goes out slowly.* AUSTEN *hums a tune to himself for a second or so.*
THELMA *knocks on Warren's hatch.*)
THELMA: (*Her voice*) Warren . . . Warren . . .
WARREN: (*Irritably*) Yes?
THELMA: Do want anything to eat, dear?
WARREN: No.
THELMA: Anything to drink? A little hot drink?
WARREN: No. No, thank you.
THELMA: Anything at all?
WARREN: (*Shouting*) No, nothing. Nothing at all, Mother.
(*Silence.*)
THELMA: (*Very hurt*) I'll say a little prayer for you, son.
(WARREN *sits on his bed in a state of extreme disquiet.*
There is a sudden knocking on Rick's basement door. RICK
gets up at once, throwing aside the duvet. She opens the door.)
RICK: (*As she does so*) At last. What time do you call this, then – ?
(RICK *has barely unlocked the door when it is forced open from
the other side and* LARRY, *a powerful man in his mid-thirties,
steps in, slams it shut, locks it and removes the key which he
pockets.* RICK, *alarmed.*)
Who the hell are – ?
LARRY: Where is she, then?
RICK: (*Outraged*) What do you think you're doing?
LARRY: Where is she? Come on. I know she's here.
(*Moving into the room*) Marcie! Marcie!
RICK: Look, what are you doing, there's nobody here.
THELMA: Don't tell me that. I've seen you both together. I saw
you this evening, going out with her on your bike. Where is
she?
RICK: She's not here. There's nobody here. You get out. Before I
call somebody.
LARRY: Christ, this place is a tip. What are you – squatting?
RICK: No, I'm not. None of your business.
LARRY: (*Looking further down the cellar*) Where's this lead?
RICK: (*Barring his way*) That is private property. Now get out. I
tell you, she's not here.

43

LARRY: Listen, darling. I'm not stupid. (*Indicating*) Two little crash helmets, two little heads, all right? I can count. Now get out of my way.

RICK: You go down there and I'll – I warn you –

(LARRY *makes to move further off down the cellar.* RICK *attempts a rather hasty, ill-aimed karate punch.* LARRY, *with consummate ease, grabs both her wrists, pulls her to him and forces both arms up behind her back.* RICK *gasps with pain.*)

LARRY: (*Very quietly, his face an inch from hers*) You ever, ever try that again and I will break both your arms. All right?

(RICK *moans.* LARRY, *applying more pressure*)

All right?

RICK *reacts but refuses to scream.*)

RICK: (*Then, in a whisper*) Yes . . .

(LARRY *half carries her and seats her quite gently but firmly on the bed before releasing her. He pushes her gently back and lifts her feet so she is lying full out.* RICK *keeps her eyes fixed on him. She is literally frozen with fright.* LARRY *picks the duvet off the floor and covers her with it. Just Rick's eyes peer out over the top of the cover.*)

LARRY: (*Softly, his face close to hers*) You lie there – absolutely still, do you hear? While I go and find my wife. (*He moves away, then turns suddenly.*) Don't move. Or I will get cross. OK? Good girl.

(LARRY *goes off down into the cellar.* RICK *lies motionless, trying to follow him with her eyes.*

AUSTEN *finishes reading the paper and crosses to the table. He sits before he notices the empty plate.*)

AUSTEN: They've eaten all my sandwiches . . .

(*Meanwhile,* THELMA *knocks on Warren's trap door.*

Under the next AUSTEN *disgustedly leaves the room, taking his plate and newspaper with him.*)

THELMA: (*Her voice*) Warren . . . Warren, dear . . .

WARREN: (*Groaning*) Oh, Mother. What now?

THELMA: It's a woman to see you, Warren.

WARREN: (*Alarmed*) A what?

THELMA: A young woman. A girl.

WARREN: Who? Who is it?

44

MARCIE: (*Her voice*) It's me, Warren. It's Marcie.

WARREN: (*Incredulous*) Marcie?

MARCIE: Could I see you just for a second?

WARREN: (*Bounding up*) Just a second. (*He attempts to tidy himself up and open the hatch simultaneously.*)

MARCIE: Hallo. May I come up?

WARREN: Yes. Yes, of course.

MARCIE: (*Her head appearing, calling down*) Thank you very much, Mrs Wrigley.

THELMA: (*Her voice*) Not at all. (*Anxiously*) Will you be all right, Warren?

WARREN: Yes, I'm fine, Mother. It's OK. It's OK. Don't worry.

THELMA: (*Doubtfully*) Yes.

WARREN: (*Helping* MARCIE *through*) Here . . .

MARCIE: Thank you.

THELMA: Warren . . .

WARREN: What is it, Mother . . .?

THELMA: You're not going to fall from grace, are you, son?

WARREN: (*Agonized*) Mother!

(*He slams shut the hatch, then realizes that* MARCIE *is staring at him, slightly startled.*)

I'm sorry. It's just she . . .

MARCIE: I know –

WARREN: It's not that I . . .

MARCIE: I understand.

WARREN: You do?

MARCIE: Absolutely.

WARREN: Ah!

MARCIE: I brought your manuscript. You left it at Mr Inchbridge's.

WARREN: Oh, thank you. Thanks very much. (*Offering her the chair*) Won't you . . .?

MARCIE: Thank you.

(MARCIE *sits.* WARREN *sits on the bed.* MARCIE *looks at him and smiles.* WARREN *smiles weakly back. He is terrified. An awkward silence.*

Meanwhile, at Rick's, LARRY *returns from the basement.* RICK *is still lying motionless, watching him.*

45

LARRY: (*Looking up the stairs*) All right, she's up here then, is she? (*He makes to climb the stairs.*)

RICK: (*Sitting up, alarmed*) No . . .

LARRY: (*Wheeling sharply*) Lie still!

(RICK *lies back immediately,* LARRY, *quieter*)

Not a twitch. Not a whisper. All right? (*A fraction louder*) All right?

RICK: (*In a whisper*) Right . . .

(*She watches* LARRY *as he goes upstairs but doesn't move again. Meanwhile,* MARCIE *breaks the silence at last.*)

MARCIE: Isn't it amazing up here? What a room. (*She smiles.*) I hope you don't mind. I read it. On my way here. Your statement.

WARREN: Oh.

MARCIE: Do you mind?

WARREN: No.

MARCIE: I just – sat in this bus shelter – waiting for this taxi – and I couldn't put it down. I only meant to look at the first page, really – but I got – I was going to return it tomorrow but once I'd read it I just had to – I mean, I didn't read it that carefully, I skimmed through a bit – but I think it's simply wonderful.

WARREN: You do?

MARCIE: Absolutely riveting. You must have the most brilliant, fantastic, imaginative, fertile brain I've ever met.

WARREN: Thank you.

MARCIE: I mean, your imagination is extraordinary. I knew it must be – from that game but . . . but this . . .

WARREN: That's all true.

MARCIE: What?

WARREN: That – what I've written there. It's true.

MARCIE: True?

WARREN: Every word. I swear it. Promise.

MARCIE: (*Breathless*) True? You mean, you're really . . . You really believe you're . . .

WARREN: I am.

MARCIE: (*In a whisper*) An alien?

WARREN: Yes.

46

MARCIE: (*Quieter still*) Golly! (*She stares at him.*) I'd like to read it again. Would you mind?

WARREN: No. Take it home.

MARCIE: No. Here, now. I have to read it now.

(LARRY *comes back down the stairs.* RICK *lying under the duvet as before.*)

LARRY: It is a stinking, disgusting sewer up there, isn't it? When did you last clean it? Eh? Revolting. Stomach-turning, that is. Some people. Animals. You're a little animal, aren't you? Like her. I thought women always prided themselves on being the clean ones. Revolting. (*He goes to the door.*) Right. Here. (*He beckons her.* RICK *does not move.*)

Come on. Come here. Or do you want me to come to you? (RICK *gets out of bed and pads over to* LARRY.)

You give my wife a message. You tell her I called, that I'm sorry I missed her and that I will be back. You got that? (RICK *nods.*)

Good girl.

(*He unlocks the door with the mortise key. He removes the key and holds it out.* RICK *makes to take it.*)

No, no. (*Indicating her mouth*) Open. Come on, open wide. (RICK *does so.* LARRY *puts the key into her mouth so that just the end sticks out.*)

I want this door left unlocked at all times. Understood? If I ever come back and find it locked, I will cause you to swallow that key. OK?

(RICK *nods.*)

That's it. Back to bed, then.

(RICK *goes back to bed, the key still in her mouth.* LARRY *switches off the light.*)

Sleep tight. Remember, I won't be far away.

(LARRY *closes the door. In the darkness,* RICK *allows herself a soft cry as she lies in the darkness.*

STANLEY, *now dressed for bed, comes into the sitting room and stands in the darkened room by the window.*

MARCIE *finishes the manuscript. She looks up.* WARREN *is snoring softly on the bed.* MARCIE *smiles. Carefully, she lays*

*down the script and tiptoeing to the hatch, unbolts it and prepares
to leave.* WARREN *jolts awake.*)

WARREN: (*Sleepily*) Marcie?

MARCIE: (*In a whisper*) Good-night, Warren.

WARREN: Did you . . .?

MARCIE: Yes, I did?

WARREN: Did you . . .?

MARCIE: It's so exciting, Warren, it has to be true.

WARREN: You're the only one who believes, you know. The only
one.

MARCIE: I believe in you, Warren . . .

WARREN: Marcie – it's just possible . . . It's very possible that you
could – you could be . . .

MARCIE: An alien as well. The same as you?

WARREN: No, you're not a Lak, like me. Not from Lakkos but
somewhere – I think – I'll have to check. I'll do some
checking. I'll let you know . . .

MARCIE: Yes, please. Do. Good-night. (*She starts to climb through
the hatch.*)

WARREN: Good-night, Marcie.

MARCIE: Warren . . .

WARREN: What?

MARCIE: However much you feel you are, you're not alone,
Warren. Never feel you're entirely alone . . . (*She gives him a
final smile and goes, closing the hatch behind her.*)

WARREN: (*To himself, excitedly*) She is. She's one of us. She must
be . . . (*He lies back on the bed in great excitement but soon gets
overtaken by sleep. The hatch slowly opens again.* WARREN *sits
up excitedly. In a whisper*) Marcie?
(*A small portion of* THELMA *peeps through the quarter-open
hatchway.*)

THELMA: I prayed for you, son, I was praying for you . . .
(*The hatch closes. Furious,* WARREN *crosses and bolts it.
At the Inchbridges',* HAZEL *in her dressing gown, looks into
the sitting room and sees* STANLEY.)

HAZEL: Stanley, what are you doing?

STANLEY: Nothing, I was just . . .

HAZEL: It's twenty-past three . . .

STANLEY: Sorry.

HAZEL: Well, come to bed. I can't sleep when you're not in bed, you know that.

STANLEY: Sorry, I'll . . . Sorry. (*He turns to follow her.*)

HAZEL: There's no point in losing sleep dreaming about her, is there? If you want her, for God's sake have her, but have a little consideration for me as well.

STANLEY: Oh, Hazel . . .

HAZEL: Come on. Upstairs.

STANLEY: You're going to drive me to it at this rate, you know, Hazel. You really are.

HAZEL: (*As she goes*) Me? Oh, that's a new one, I must say . . .

STANLEY: (*As he goes*) Hazel . . .

(*They have both gone.*
There is a soft knocking on Rick's basement door. The handle is tried, the door is pushed open. Marcie's face cautiously appears.)

MARCIE: Rick . . . Rick . . . Rick, are you all right? Rick.
(RICK *moans from her bed.* MARCIE, *hearing her*)
Oh, dear God! (MARCIE *closes the door and crosses to the bed.*)
What's happened, Rick? What's happened, darling?
(MARCIE *sits on the bed and clasps* RICK *to her.*)
What's the matter? Tell me?
(RICK *makes a gurgling sound.*)
What are you doing – with this . . . What are you doing with this in your mouth?
(MARCIE *pulls out the key.* RICK *gives a great sob.*)
Has he been here? Was this Larry? Did you let him in? Why the hell did you let him in?

RICK: (*Sobbing*) I – thought – it – was – you . . .

MARCIE: What did he do? Did he hurt you?

RICK: No . . .

MARCIE: Then what . . .?

RICK: (*Almost inaudibly, her breath coming in great gasps*) I – was – just – so – frightened . . .

MARCIE: What? What's that?

RICK: Frightened. I – wanted – to – be – so – brave – for – you – and – I was just – shit – scared . . .

49

MARCIE: Shit scared? Yes. Well, I know how you feel. Why do you think I ran away from him?

RICK: But – I wanted – to – be brave . . .

MARCIE: (*Soothing her*) Yes OK. OK. And I need you to be brave, Rick. You see? I need you to be brave for me, my darling. Do you see? I need you. I need your courage. All right? Yes?

RICK: (*Recovering slightly*) Yes.

MARCIE: I need Herwin. I need my warrior to look after me. OK?

RICK: Yes. (*She wriggles free of* MARCIE *and climbs off the bed and marches to the door.*)

MARCIE: (*Slightly alarmed*) Where are you going?

RICK: I'm going to lock this door. If he tries to get in again, I'll kill the bastard.

(*A swift cross-fade to the Inchbridges' sitting room.* STANLEY *enters in a much more positive mood than usual. He goes to the sideboard and, taking out the game, starts to lay it out on the table as before.*)

STANLEY: (*Calling, as he does this*) All right, all right, everyone. If we're all here we ought to get started. We've got a lot to get through this evening. There are battles to be fought and won . . . come on in. Come through. (*Finding he has a figure missing*) That's odd . . . Where's Idonia?

(HAZEL *enters with the anglepoise. She seems to have sharpened her image slightly. Maybe it's the new dress.*)

Hazel, I've lost Idonia. Have you seen her?

HAZEL: Oh, yes. I – I've re-dressed her.

STANLEY: Re-dressed? How do you mean?

HAZEL: (*As she fixes the lamp*) I felt she needed a change of image.

STANLEY: Really? I thought she looked fine. Where is she?

(*At this moment,* WARREN *comes in with a couple of chairs and* RICK *with a third. They place these around the table. The whole group has an excitement, a tension about it.*)

Right. Quick as we can, well done. We must get started. Sit down, everyone.

(*They all sit.* HAZEL *has the 'new-look' Idonia with her but, at present, keeps this figure hidden.*)

Got the parameters, Warren?

WARREN: Yes. But we know where we're going.

STANLEY: Yes. This time to Balaac. Where's Marcie?

RICK: She was in the bathroom. She's just coming.

STANLEY: Do the lights for us, Warren, will you?

WARREN: Yes, Mr Inchbridge . . .

> (*Even as he starts to rise* MARCIE *enters and does the job for him.*)

MARCIE: I'll do it. (MARCIE *appears more excited than any of them.*) Sorry. Off we go then. Hallo, Warren.

WARREN: Hallo. (*Hastily whispering to her*) I think I've got some great news for you . . .

MARCIE: (*Whispering back*) What?

STANLEY: Oh, we need the salt-cellar again. (*To* HAZEL) We need Marcie's salt-cellar, dear.

MARCIE: No, that's OK. There! (*She puts a small figure she has been holding down on the board. Hers is attractive, a little like a character from 'Flash Gordon' or a more exotic episode of 'Star Trek'.*) Brought my own this week.

STANLEY: Oh, that's lovely.

WARREN: Terrific.

RICK: Great.

STANLEY: Isn't that beautiful, Hazel?

HAZEL: Yes. There! (*She puts down her new 'Idonia' figure next to Marcie's. Hazel's tends to the romantic, even younger than before – a long frock and flowing hair. There is a definite contest in prospect.*)

STANLEY: Good heavens, just look at that.

WARREN: Ah.

MARCIE: How lovely. Simply lovely. Congratulations. Did you make it yourself, Hazel?

HAZEL: (*Smugly*) Yes, I did.

MARCIE: I wish I was that clever with my hands.

HAZEL: I expect you can be when you need to be.

> (MARCIE *looks rather puzzled.*)

STANLEY: Right, everyone. Concentration. We must now set out on what might well be our final journey of the game. To death or victory.

WARREN: Death or victory!

ALL: Death or victory!

STANLEY: To the south, then . . . Onward . . .
> (*They move their pieces, one by one, across the board, step by step.*)
>
> Are you ready and armed, Herwin?

RICK: Ready and armed, Wise One.

STANLEY: What do you sense. Idonia child . . .?

HAZEL: Hurdle-murre-durne . . . I sense great danger, Wise One . . .

STANLEY: What do you see and hear, Xenon, the Stranger?

WARREN: I hear Balaac. I do not yet see him. He is distant but approaching slowly.

STANLEY: Good. Onward!

HAZEL: Onward!

WARREN: Onward!

RICK: Onward!

MARCIE: (*Excitedly*) Onward!

STANLEY: What can you report now?

HAZEL: Troodle-smaire-hart . . . The danger increases still more, Wise One. Clouds are gathering. There is impenetrable darkness ahead.

WARREN: Balaac has sensed our presence. He is starting to approach more rapidly. I cannot yet see him.
> (*The sound of a wind can be faintly heard now.*)

STANLEY: Onward!

HAZEL: Onward!

WARREN: Onward!

RICK: Onward!

MARCIE: (*Goading them on*) Onward!

HAZEL: Broochj! Broochj! There is a wind. A terrible storm approaching. And with it comes deep, deep evil.

WARREN: Balaac is approaching very fast now. He is riding the very wind itself . . .
> (*Under the next the wind effect starts and crescendos.*)

STANLEY: Onward!

HAZEL: Onward!

WARREN: Onward!

RICK: Onward!

MARCIE: (*Almost screaming with excitement*) Onward!

HAZEL: Oorspickle-gerdiff . . . He rides with the storm. The
lightning is his bridle and his hoofs are the thunder . . .
WARREN: He's very close, very close now, but I still can't see him
. . . Where is he? Where is he? Why can't I see him?
(*They are all now having to shout over the wind.*)
STANLEY: Ready, Herwin?
RICK: Ready. I'm ready . . . Let him come . . .
(*A growing thunderous roar building to a wail.*)
WARREN: He's here, he's here . . . He's here amongst us . . . Why
can't we see him . . .?
HAZEL: Oh, my God, what's happening, what's happening . . .?
STANLEY: Stay calm, everybody . . .
(RICK *gives a great war-like yell, stands and raises her arms
above her head.* MARCIE *yells.* HAZEL *screams. There is a
sudden, final thunderous explosion as if the devil's hoofbeats had
ridden over them.* RICK *sits. Silence.*)
HAZEL: (*After a moment, nervously in a small voice — half Idonia's,
half her own*) What's happening to us? What's happening?
Stanley . . .?
WARREN: Wise One?
STANLEY: — er . . . I'm . . . I'm . . .
(*They are all looking at him, expectantly.* STANLEY, *pulling
himself together*)
. . . er . . . fear not, friends. (*More confidently*) Fear not. (*With
sudden authority*) Fear not!
MARCIE: (*Her face radiant from the experience*) Fantastic!
(*Blackout.*)

ACT II

The same. A few days later. In the basement, RICK *is preparing a meal. It is hardly a banquet but at least it's an effort. Marcie's influence is here seen at work. The room, too, has taken on a generally tidier appearance.*

We will see RICK *from time to time during the next, as we will* WARREN, *who is busily installing a great deal more wiring. This entails him appearing and disappearing through his hatchway at odd intervals as he pays out cable from a drum. The cables in turn are connected via a mixer to his computer system.*

At the Inchbridges', STANLEY *enters breathlessly. He carries a small package. He is cheerful and positive. He is followed by* MARCIE, *who is laughing. They both slump in chairs, exhausted*

STANLEY: What on earth have you bought? What have you been buying, woman?

MARCIE: (*Excitedly*) Oh, everything. Don't ask. Everything. Lucky I met you, wasn't it? I can't even remember half the things now. I bought the shop. I'm hopeless. I just see things, I want them, I can't afford them but I buy them. I just love Christmas, don't you? I love giving presents. My whole family are like that. We all used to give each other ten presents each. When I was a kid on Christmas morning you could barely see the Christmas tree. Just this mountain of wrapping paper.

STANLEY: Do you have a large family?

MARCIE: Two sisters, a brother. My mother, father. Uncles and aunts and cousins and things. Quite big.

STANLEY: Will you be going home for Christmas?

MARCIE: (*Frowning slightly*) No. Not this year.

(*In the basement,* RICK *comes on to lay the table. Two bowls, two spoons, new salt- and pepper-mills.*

(MARCIE, *slight pause*) We – my father doesn't – isn't talking to me. He didn't approve of my marriage.

STANLEY: I thought you said that was over.

MARCIE: It is.

STANLEY: Well?

MARCIE: No. They wouldn't approve of that either. It's difficult. They're – very conventional people.

STANLEY: Ah.

(RICK *goes off again.*)

What do they do?

MARCIE: My father's an MP.

STANLEY: (*Impressed*) Is he?

MARCIE: Not a very important one.

STANLEY: Oh.

MARCIE: So's my mother.

STANLEY: An MP?

MARCIE: Yes. She's slightly more important. She's a shadow something. I forget.

STANLEY: Oh. And do they – ?

MARCIE: (*Restlessly*) I don't think I want to talk about me any more, do you mind?

STANLEY: No, of course. I'm sorry. I was just . . .

(MARCIE *rises and paces about.*

WARREN *in his attic appears and in due course disappears, busy with his wiring.*)

MARCIE: Will my stuff be all right in the hall there?

STANLEY: Yes, sure. Hazel must still be out. And Austen won't be back for a little bit. Sit down.

MARCIE: I'll go in a minute. When I've got my breath back.

STANLEY: How will you get home with all that?

MARCIE: I can get a taxi from the corner. (*Looking around*) I haven't been here since – since the night we played the game.

STANLEY: Not that long ago. Less than a week.

MARCIE: Wasn't it extraordinary? It couldn't really have been a freak storm, could it? I know that's what we all agreed it had to be – but it must have been more than that. What do you think it was?

STANLEY: (*The schoolteacher*) I think it might – well – I believe it could have been an accumulation – a sort of freak gathering of a great deal of psychic energy. I think as a group we must have been giving off an abnormal amount. For some reason.

And maybe – like a capacitor – an electrical capacitor does – our combined energies reached a level where they simply discharged . . . I mean, that's just a theory.

MARCIE: It sounds a good one to me . . .

STANLEY: I don't think you'd get many scientists to believe it.

MARCIE: (*Dismissively*) Scientists? What do they know? I'd sooner listen to someone like you. Someone who relates things to people, even if they're wrong.

STANLEY: (*Doubtfully*) Well, thank you.

MARCIE: I bet you're a marvellous teacher.

STANLEY: Well . . .

MARCIE: I wish you'd taught me. My teachers were all – awful. Dull. Dead. I don't think any of them had been outside the school building since 1950.

STANLEY: Where were you educated?

MARCIE: (*Evasive again*) Oh, you wouldn't know it – let's not talk about me, please. I hate it.

STANLEY: Why not? I'm interested.

MARCIE: In me?

STANLEY: Yes.

MARCIE: I'm not very interesting.

STANLEY: You're very interesting.

MARCIE: Am I?

STANLEY: Very. I want to know all about you.

MARCIE: Perhaps. One day. Not now.

(RICK *returns, stirring a saucepan of thick soup. She tastes it, wrinkles her nose and adds salt from the salt-mill*).

Will you carry on playing the game?

STANLEY: Probably. (*Only half joking*) If you'll promise to come, that is.

MARCIE: I don't think I should, you know. Seriously.

STANLEY: Why not?

MARCIE: I'm not one of the group, am I? Not really.

STANLEY: You are.

MARCIE: I don't think some of you feel I am.

STANLEY: Who?

MARCIE: Well – Hazel, really.

STANLEY: Ah.

MARCIE: I don't know why she doesn't like me but she doesn't. I can't think what I'm supposed to have done, can you?

STANLEY: (*A little guiltily*) No.

MARCIE: Well, can you? I can't think what. Sometimes I just seem to do that to people.

STANLEY: You've done nothing.

MARCIE: It's a pity. I like her. I think we could have been really, really friendly. Still . . . Maybe she's more of a man's woman. Do you think that's it?

STANLEY: (*Doubtfully*) No. I wouldn't have described her as that.

MARCIE: It must be me, then. Never mind. It happens. There was a girl at school like that. But I found out later it was because I stole her best friend.

STANLEY: Ah.

MARCIE: Did you have a best friend?

STANLEY: At school?

MARCIE: Yes.

STANLEY: Yes, I think so. It was – rather a long time ago.

MARCIE: I had hundreds. I love having friends.

(*At this point,* HAZEL *comes in. She is in her coat and has obviously just arrived home. She has had her hair done. She looks a lot younger. Her manner, too, is bright and chirpy – if a little brittle.*)

HAZEL: (*As she enters*) . . . what on earth is all that stuff in the hall? Who's been . . . (*Seeing them both.*) Whoops! Sorry, beg your pardon! (*She goes out again. Off, along the hall.*) Sorry! Sorry!

STANLEY: (*Vainly*) Hazel!

HAZEL: (*Distant*) Sorry!

STANLEY: (*Embarrassed, to* MARCIE) Sorry.

MARCIE: She's had her hair done differently.

STANLEY: Yes. Has she?

MARCIE: Suits her. It's much nicer.

STANLEY: I'll – tell her.

MARCIE: You should. Women like to be told. It shows you've noticed them.

STANLEY: Yes.

(*A pause.* WARREN *reappears again with more wire. He disappears in due course.*)

57

Your hair's nice. I always think.

MARCIE: *My* hair?

STANLEY: Yes.

MARCIE: My hair's horrible. I loathe my hair. If we're going to start discussing my hair, I'm off.

(*She has risen again.* STANLEY *follows suit.* AUSTEN *enters with the evening paper.*)

AUSTEN: (*As he enters*) . . . what's all that – (*Seeing them.*) Ah! Good-evening. Good-evening, Marcie.

MARCIE: 'evening, Mr Skate.

AUSTEN: Is that your accumulation of purchases out there on the floor, is it?

MARCIE: Yes, I'm sorry.

AUSTEN: I nearly had occasion to fall over them, did you know that?

MARCIE: I'm very sorry.

AUSTEN: Never, young lady, on any account leave obstructions in a passageway. It's very dangerous. You should know that.

STANLEY: She's just off . . .

AUSTEN: Are you cognizant with the percentage of accidents that occur in the home?

MARCIE: No. Lots, I imagine.

AUSTEN: Would you care to hazard a guess?

STANLEY: Austen, Marcie's going now . . .

AUSTEN: Well, may I suggest that the next time, young lady, the next time you contemplate depositing a positive pile, a huge hummock, a massive mountain, a considerable cumulus of stuff about the place, you stop and spare a thought for other people. Enough said?

MARCIE: (*Chastened*) Sorry, Mr Skate.

STANLEY: Tumulus.

AUSTEN: Eh?

STANLEY: Tumulus. You said cumulus. I think you meant tumulus. Tumulus is a mound, originally a burial mound. Whereas cumulus is a rain cloud. Sorry to correct you, Austen, but I know how punctilious you are about those sort of things.

(AUSTEN *stares at him in amazement.*)

You know that word, punctilious? It means precise observation to detail; exact attention to form; nit-picking.
(STANLEY *and* MARCIE *go out.* AUSTEN *sits slowly.*

RICK returns with the pan again. She tastes the soup with disapproval and decides to grind in some pepper.

As she does this, WARREN *returns to his room and sits at the console. He switches on his screen. A beeping sound is heard.*)

WARREN: (*Muttering*) Great. Great. Gotcher.

(*He sets to work, connecting the wires he has run to the console.*

Meanwhile, STANLEY *has wandered back into the sitting room. He picks up his package and is about to go out when* HAZEL *bounces in.*)

HAZEL: (*Brightly*) Oh – has she gone? What a pity, I was going to make us all some tea. Never mind. She'll be popping in again before long, I expect. Won't she?

(*She goes out again, singing loudly with more volume than tune. We hear her in the kitchen, crashing about.*

STANLEY *stares after her rather despairingly. He sees* AUSTEN *looking at him over the top of his newspaper.* STANLEY *shrugs rather ineffectually. This seems to be the final straw as far as* AUSTEN's *concerned. He folds up the paper and lays it down.*

STANLEY *starts to leave the room.*)

AUSTEN: (*Sharply*) Just a minute!

STANLEY: (*Startled*) What?

AUSTEN: (*Rising*) Just a minute. Just a minute. (*Pause.*) Just a minute.

(AUSTEN *gathers his thoughts.* STANLEY *waits.* HAZEL *sings on in the kitchen.*)

I presume you are aware that you are driving my sister to the brink of a nervous breakdown? Are you aware of that fact?

STANLEY: Rubbish.

AUSTEN: It is a fact. Listen.

(*They listen.* HAZEL *sings.*)

Correct me if I'm wrong, but isn't that the sound of a woman losing her reason?

STANLEY: It's the sound of a woman singing.

AUSTEN: (*Shouting angrily*) No, it isn't. Not any woman. That is the sound of *Hazel* singing. My sister. Hazel never used to

59

sing like that. Hazel never used to sing at all. All through
our childhood I never remember her singing. Hazel is tone-
deaf. Like all our family. I am telling you for a fact,
Inchbridge, that is the sound of a woman in mental
torment. That is the sound of a woman driven to
desperation by a husband flaunting his whores and
peccadilloes right under his own wife's nose in her own
front room.

STANLEY: How dare you?

AUSTEN: Don't interrupt me. I am warning you, Inchbridge, if
my sister loses one iota of her mental stability because of
your moral misdemeanours, I will have you in court, so
help me I will.

STANLEY: In court? On what grounds?

AUSTEN: (*Beside himself with fury*) On the grounds that you are a
bastard, that's why. A lecherous, insensitive, died-in-the-
wool bastard! Have you anything to say for yourself,
anything?

STANLEY: (*Looking at him for a second*) Oh, get stuffed, Austen.
If anyone's driven her barmy, it's you. You've driven us
both round the bend. You saw your own wife off and then
started on us.

AUSTEN: How dare you insinuate that about my wife. Mary died
in considerable pain . . .

STANLEY: Mary died with indecent haste. She couldn't wait to
get shot of you, poor cow . . .

AUSTEN: You will retract that statement immediately.

STANLEY: You got shot of her and then you started on us. And,
by God, you've succeeded. You've hounded us, Austen.
You've hovered over our marriage like some bloody great
stuffed albatross.

AUSTEN: I'm noting all this down, Inchbridge, never fear.

STANLEY: Hazel and I have never had a moment to ourselves
since the day we were married. We could never even make
love properly because you were listening at the door . . .

AUSTEN: That's a lie, I never stooped to that —

STANLEY: We could hear you, Austen, we heard you stooping
and breathing and wheezing through our bedroom keyhole.

60

We could never be properly alone anywhere. Not in the house. Anywhere. You even sat behind us in the cinema . . .

AUSTEN: That was pure coincidence and you know it . . .

STANLEY: What, in Norwich? That was supposedly our honeymoon, Austen. Two weeks on the Broads and you waiting at every bloody lock with a movie camera . . .

AUSTEN: All right, so I cared about Hazel. I worried for her. I'm not ashamed of that . . .

STANLEY: (*Ploughing on*) . . . every time we tried to talk to each other you sat there correcting our grammar – you've had us waiting on you hand and foot for fifteen years and we've never had one word of thanks. You've treated me like a lodger and Hazel like a housekeeper. Anything that's happened in this house is entirely due to you, Austen . . . You're the reason that's going on out there . . .

AUSTEN: Oh, no, the reason for that . . . I'll tell you in one word the reason for that. Betrayal. You have betrayed my sister, Inchbridge.

STANLEY: Oh, don't be so bloody melodramatic . . .

AUSTEN: You've thrown her over for some passing piece of skirt half your age and left her with nothing. You weren't man enough even to give Hazel children.

STANLEY: (*Low*) I rather left that to you, Austen. I thought you considered that your job.

(*Silence. Even* HAZEL *has stopped singing.*)

AUSTEN: (*Quietly*) Get out. Get out of this house. (*He appears to be having trouble breathing.*) Do you hear me? I want you out. Out, now. You will not make allegations of that nature and stay under my roof.

STANLEY: OK. Fine. OK.

AUSTEN: You haven't heard the end of this. Oh, no. No. I have ways. Don't worry. I have ways. Make no mistake, we haven't yet finished with this little matter, you and me.

STANLEY: I.

AUSTEN: What?

STANLEY: You and I. You said you and me. You and I.

(AUSTEN *opens and shuts his mouth and looks as if he might explode.*)

AUSTEN: I'm going upstairs to my room. By the time I come down, I want you out of this house, all right?

STANLEY: Suits me.

(AUSTEN *goes out. He looks distinctly shaky.* STANLEY *stands and watches him.*

RICK *returns with her saucepan and tries more salt.*

WARREN *labours on in his attic. He appears to be nearing completion.*

HAZEL *comes in with a jam-jar full of flowers. She puts them on the table and stands back to admire them.*)

HAZEL: There. Don't they look pretty?

STANLEY: Yes. Hazel, those are dandelions.

HAZEL: I know. I picked them for your little friend. I thought they might make her wet the bed. (*She giggles.*) Doodle-addle-doodle-oodle . . . (*She goes out.*)

STANLEY: (*Appalled*) Oh, my God. What have I done?

(*At* WARREN's, *because the hatchway is open, we hear the front doorbell ring.* WARREN *stops what he is doing and turns up his computer-screen volume. The beeping sound as before.* WARREN *studies the screen intently. The beeping gets more rapid. Then we hear Thelma's voice from the bottom of the ladder.*)

THELMA: (*Her voice*) Warren, Warren, dear . . .

(WARREN *turns down his volume.*

STANLEY *goes off during the next.*)

WARREN: What is it, Mother?

THELMA: There's that young woman here again, Warren . . .

WARREN: Well, show her up, Mother, show her up.

THELMA: She's come in a taxi, Warren.

WARREN: Yes, all right.

THELMA: (*Filled with foreboding*) Oh, son. I hope you're allowing the Lord to guide your footsteps.

WARREN: Every inch of the way, Mother. Will you let her in?

THELMA: You are going to tidy all this wire up soon, aren't you, dear?

WARREN: Yes, Mother. Don't touch anything.

THELMA: (*Her voice receding*) Only someone's going to trip over it . . .

(WARREN *turns up the volume and studies the screen for a second. There are now double beeps.*)

MARCIE: (*Her voice*) Warren, it's me. Marcie. May I come up?

WARREN: (*Turning down the screen again*) Yes, sure.
   (*Marcie's head appears through the hatch. She is carrying a book.*)

MARCIE: What on earth are you doing? The house is full of wires. It's like a snake-pit. I brought you back your book.
   (*Climbing up.*) What's going on? Are you building something special? (*As* WARREN *helps her through.*) Thanks.

WARREN: (*Secretively*) It's nothing. Just security.

MARCIE: Security?
   (WARREN *closes the hatch*).

WARREN: What did you make of the book?

MARCIE: Oh, Mr Van der Hooch. Fantastic.

WARREN: But true, though.

MARCIE: Well . . .

WARREN: He spent twenty years of his life on that, you know.

MARCIE: Yes, I read.

WARREN: He wouldn't have given up a university career like he had for nothing, would he . . .?

MARCIE: Yes, but I thought they –

WARREN: What?

MARCIE: I thought they – sort of sacked him . . .

WARREN: And did you read why?

MARCIE: – er . . . for falsifying results, wasn't it?

WARREN: No, no, no. Wrong.

MARCIE: Ah. I thought . . .

WARREN: For arriving at results that threw all other accepted conventionally held theories out of the window. Not just the laws of physics, but chemistry, astronomy, biology, even gravity . . .

MARCIE: Yes, I see.

WARREN: Electromagnetics, relativity. Arnie stood them all on their head. And for that they hounded him . . .

MARCIE: Yes.

WARREN: He lived in a hut on nothing but raw reindeer meat for twenty years, you know . . .

MARCIE: That doesn't sound too good. (*Slight pause.*) Is your mother all right? She looks a bit –

WARREN: Oh, she'll be fine. It's just that we are going through a critical phase at present. She and I.

MARCIE: How do you mean?

WARREN: Well, as I told you, she is an Orgue. They are a hardy species, very loyal but of limited intelligence. They are used on Lakkos – which is where I am originally from, of course – I am a Lak –

MARCIE: Yes, I know . . .

WARREN: – the Laks, being of a higher intelligence, use the Orgues to mind their children until the young Lak reaches maturity. At this point in the relationship, the Orgue ceases to be important and the Lak becomes naturally dominant.

MARCIE: Yes, I see. Complicated. What happens to the poor old Orgue?

WARREN: Ah, well. They are either discarded or occasionally they're kept as pets.

MARCIE: Well, I hope maybe you'll hang on to your mother.

WARREN: Possibly. We'll see. We'll see.

MARCIE: (*Gently*) When is it you – when do you expect to reach this maturity, then, Warren?

WARREN: Any day now I will undergo a change – during which I must keep my mother away and then, *voilà*.

MARCIE: Will you – look any different?

WARREN: Not – to the naked eye. But . . . to certain people, yes.

MARCIE: Who? Like who?

WARREN: (*Deciding this is the moment*) Well, this is the news I wanted to tell you. I think, Marcie, that you're almost certainly a Trilla.

MARCIE: A Trilla? Me? What's a Trilla?

WARREN: T – R – I – double L – A.

MARCIE: How pretty.

WARREN: They are. They're some of the most beautiful beings in the universe. In your natural state you'd be even more incredibly beautiful than you are now.

MARCIE: My natural state?

WARREN: Stripped of your humanoid characteristics.

MARCIE: Oh, I see.

WARREN: The point is – this is the exciting bit – the Trillas and the Laks were once one being. They had a symbiotic relationship. But they were split apart at the crash.

MARCIE: I see, I see.

WARREN: But once in a while, by chance, both halves get reunited and together they become the most beautiful and powerful creature in the universe. Arnie told of a dream he once had, long ago, in which a Trilla visited him. And she floated at the foot of his bed and divested herself of her coverings till she was naked for him. And Arnie said it was at that moment that he experienced that deep pain that could only be sensed through the deepest pleasure.

MARCIE: Ah.

WARREN: Now it's very possible that once I've – you know – changed – we might both recognize that beauty in each other . . . (*He moves closer.*)

MARCIE: (*Rising*) Yes. I've got this taxi waiting at the moment, Warren, so I won't . . .

WARREN: That's my hope. That would make us together something wonderful.

MARCIE: Well, we'll see. Sorry, I –

WARREN: Yes. Right. See you Thursday . . .

MARCIE: – er . . . yes. Sure. Bye.

(MARCIE *starts to climb down the ladder again.*

Under the next, HAZEL *comes into her sitting room and sits at the table. She has her needlework basket with her and is working intently on something very small. She is immensely concentrated on this, like a child.*)

WARREN: Bye.

MARCIE: Warren?

WARREN: Um?

MARCIE: Be as nice as you can to your mother, won't you?

WARREN: Oh, sure.

(MARCIE *goes.* WARREN *closes the hatch and goes quickly back to his screen. The double beeps as before.*)
She's beautiful, Arnie. You're right. She's sheer, total beauty.

(*In a moment,* WARREN *sets to work again on his wiring.*
RICK *puts more salt in her soup and goes off again.*

STANLEY *comes on rather anxiously*.)

STANLEY: (*Calling*) Hazel . . . Hazel . . . (*He stops as he sees* HAZEL *at work at the table*.)

HAZEL: (*Without looking up*) Mmm.

STANLEY: Do we – do we have Dr Blake's phone number anywhere?

HAZEL: (*Still absorbed*) It's in my address book.

STANLEY: Right. (*He looks round*.) And where's your address book?

HAZEL: In the kitchen.

STANLEY: It's just that – well, I was passing Austen's room and I heard him . . . He's lying on his bed, he's a very strange colour – and I think he's having trouble breathing . . . I think it could be a stroke – or a fit – or a heart attack . . .

HAZEL: (*Still concentrating*) Oh dear . . .

STANLEY: So I think we'd better – hadn't we? Yes. Hazel, what are you doing?

HAZEL: (*Still not looking up*) I'm making something for me . . .

STANLEY: What are you making?

HAZEL: A little dress. (*Holding up a tiny frock for a small child figure*.) Look . . .

STANLEY: Ah, yes. Lovely. (*Laughing nervously*.) A bit – small, isn't it?

HAZEL: (*Scornfully*) It's not for me, you silly. It's for Idonia. For little Idonia.

STANLEY: (*Greatly relieved*) Oh, for little Idonia. Oh, splendid! Look, I'm going to phone Blake . . . Are you going to – look in on Austen, are you?

HAZEL: (*Back to her work*) When I've finished this.

STANLEY: (*Staring at her*) Yes. Right.

(STANLEY *goes out, leaving* HAZEL *still concentrating on her task. During the next she finishes and leaves the room, taking her workbasket.*

There is a knocking on the basement door. RICK *hurries on and is about to open it but checks herself in time*.)

RICK: (*Calling*) Who is it?

MARCIE: (*Her voice*) Marcie. It's Marcie. Sorry I'm late.

RICK: (*Unlocking the door*) About time . . .

66

(*She opens the door.* MARCIE *staggers in with a couple of large carrier bags.*)

MARCIE: (*Breathless*) Sorry, I was . . . (*Calling to someone behind her.*) Thanks very much.

RICK: Who's that?

MARCIE: Taxi driver. He was a terribly nice man. He's got a son at Keele University . . . (*She dumps down the bags and returns outside for more packages.*)

RICK: You're still taking taxis . . .

MARCIE: I had to. Look at it all. Look what I've got. Give us a hand.

(*We see the extent of Marcie's shopping spree. Six similarly vast carriers and a couple of big square parcels.*)

RICK: (*Carrying things in*) What have you bought here?

MARCIE: (*Secretively*) Ha-ha! You'll have to wait till next week, won't you? Wait till Christmas.

(RICK *closes and locks the door.* MARCIE *takes off her coat and goes off briefly to hang it up.*)

RICK: (*Surveying the parcels*) How much have you spent? (*To herself.*) How much has she spent?

MARCIE: (*Off*) Mmm! What's the delicious smell? Hey! You've christened the stove! (*Returning.*) Did it work all right?

RICK: Yes. Just plugged it in.

MARCIE: Brilliant. Glad one of us is technically minded. What are you cooking?

RICK: Oh, some – soup. Sort of soup. Want to try it?

MARCIE: (*Tidying away some of her packages*) You bet. Sort of soup is just the sort of thing I could do with.

RICK: (*Going off*) I don't know what it'll be like.

MARCIE: I haven't eaten all day. (*As she speaks, she surveys the table a trifle critically. She rearranges Rick's primitive setting a little.*) Sorry I'm late. I stopped off to see Warren. He's – well, I think he's some sort of genius. He has to be. He's just – not of this world, is he?

RICK: (*Returning with the saucepan*) He's mad. (*She is about to put the pan straight on to the table.*)

MARCIE: (*Stopping her*) Hang on, don't burn the table . . .

RICK: Doesn't matter, does it?

MARCIE: (*Slipping a magazine under the pan*) Well, silly to do that. Now, what have we here? Smells wonderful. You know, I'm starving, I haven't eaten since this morning.

(RICK *serves up*.)

What we need is a tureen. Or a bowl, don't we? Yum. Do with some mats, too. (*Receiving her bowl*.) Thank you. It's home-made, isn't it? And proper soup spoons, I suppose. Eventually.

RICK: (*Sitting*) Right. Cheers.

MARCIE: Cheers!

(*Silence while they both take a mouthful or two. It's obviously revolting but* MARCIE *puts a brave face on it*.)

Golly! It's wonderful. Really unusual. Is this the first time you've made it?

RICK: (*Her eyes watering from the taste*) Yes.

MARCIE: How clever. Did you use a recipe?

RICK: (*Choking*) No.

MARCIE: Well, I think that's brilliant. I could never do that. There are some people who are just natural instinctive cooks. Give them a stove and a handful of ingredients and they can just concoct something out of thin . . . (*She tails away*.)

(*As she has been speaking,* RICK *has taken both their bowls, tipped them back into the saucepan and taken both that and the bowls back into the kitchen area. She returns and sits. Silence*.)

I wasn't really that hungry.

(*Silence*.)

You can't blame yourself if you don't get it absolutely perfectly right first time. It's very, very difficult . . .

RICK: (*Bitterly*) Unless you're an instinctive cook . . .

MARCIE: Well. Neither am I. You can't cook anything properly, anyway, on that thing. We need a proper stove.

(RICK *sits miserably*.)

I'll make us some coffee.

(MARCIE *goes off, leaving* RICK *alone*.

WARREN, *in his attic, appears to have completed another phase in his wiring programme. He opens the hatch. He has a microphone on his console with a switch, which he now presses down*.)

WARREN: (*His voice booming around the house downstairs*) This is
Warren Wrigley testing – one – two – three – four . . .
(*A distant cry of alarm from* THELMA. WARREN, *contentedly, to
himself*)
Good. Good.
THELMA: (*Her voice from below*) Warren . . . Warren . . .
WARREN: What is it, Mother?
THELMA: What's happening, Warren?
WARREN: Nothing to worry about, Mother. I was just testing.
You go back to bed.
THELMA: How did you know I was in bed?
WARREN: I know where you are at all times, Mother, remember
that. Now go to bed.
THELMA: (*Departing*) I thought it was your father. Returned to
us.
(WARREN *closes the hatch, irritated by this interruption. He
studies his master wiring diagram. Under the next, he opens the
hatch again and climbs down, clutching the diagram and
frowning.*
MARCIE *returns with two mugs of coffee.*)
MARCIE: I couldn't see any milk, I don't know if you
remembered to –
RICK: No, I forgot.
MARCIE: Oh, it doesn't matter. Better for us, anyway. (*She puts
one mug down by* RICK *and sits apart from her.*) Actually, let's
face it, what we need is a fridge, don't we? We need a lot of
things really.
(*Pause.*)
I – I might as well tell you. While you were out yesterday, I
had a look upstairs . . .
(RICK *looks at her sharply.*)
I'm sorry. I know you never want anyone to go up there but
– well, it's such a waste, isn't it? It's vast. There's those three
bedrooms and that huge sitting room and a lovely big
bathroom. And the kitchen's huge. It's a lovely room. It
could be. It's such a waste. Don't you think so, really?
(RICK *does not reply.*)
I mean, I know it would need masses doing to it, but . . . We

69

could really make it wonderful. Between us. It needn't cost a lot. It's all there. Basically.

(*Silence.*)

I'm sorry. Are you very angry with me? Why can't you go up there? Is it – because of them? Your parents? Well, your mother and – But, Rick, darling, they've gone, haven't they? They're not there now. Are they part of the dreams you have? You do know you dream, don't you? Shout out in the night. You're always doing it. (*Laughing.*) I thought the house was on fire the first night you . . .

(*Pause.*)

Actually, I must tell you – I had this awful fear that you'd . . . that they were – your parents were up there murdered or something. In a cupboard. You'd done them to death. There was this awful smell. But that just turned out to be the food. There was still this meal laid out – well, the remains of it – on the kitchen table. Was that the meal she left for you the day they . . .? Yes. Must have been. God! (*She shivers.*) Yes, I did, I read the note, as well. I'm sorry. I told you I'm a terribly nosy person. I didn't realize. Is that your real name? Alice? Alice. It's a lovely name.

(*There is still no response from* RICK. MARCIE *suddenly stands.*)

Listen. Will you do something for me? For me? Will you? Come upstairs with me. Now.

(RICK *looks at her again.* MARCIE, *holding out her hand.*)

Come on. Please. For me. Please. There's nothing there to be frightened of. No one. Trust me.

(*She takes Rick's hand. Rick allows herself to be led to the foot of the stairs.*)

Come on. That's it. I'll be with you, darling. Come on, Rick. Alice? Are you ready? OK?

RICK: (*Dully*) On one condition.

MARCIE: (*Gently*) What's that?

RICK: Never ever, ever again call me Alice . . .

MARCIE: I promise.

(*They climb the stairs slowly together.*

The lights cross-fade to the Inchbridges' sitting room.

STANLEY *hurries in with a tray plus a bottle of sherry and four*

70

glasses. From somewhere along the hall, the sound of a Christmas-carol recording. He places the tray on the sideboard and starts to pour out drinks during the next. He is followed by WARREN *with the anglepoise, which he, in turn, attaches to the table. Both men are extremely positive in manner. Indeed, the whole house tonight is filled with confidence and goodwill.*)

STANLEY: (*As he enters*) . . . might as well push the boat out a bit seeing as it's Christmas, eh?

WARREN: Very nice idea, Mr Inchbridge.

STANLEY: Warren, I really – Hazel and I really appreciate your coming round tonight – of all nights . . .

WARREN: That's all right, Mr Inchbridge . . .

STANLEY: No, I mean. Christmas Eve – you and Rick, you both would probably have preferred to spend it with your nearest and dearest. Sherry?

WARREN: Thank you very much.

STANLEY: Well, I don't think we need wait for them. Good health. Happy Christmas.

WARREN: Happy Christmas, Mr Inchbridge.
(*They drink.*)

STANLEY: Mmm. Not bad. Not too bad.

WARREN: Very nice.

STANLEY: Yes. Smooth. It has a good nose. (*Tasting again*) Mellow. Palatable. Mmmm. Mmmm?

WARREN: (*Tasting again*) Mmmm. Mmmm.

STANLEY: (*Agreeing with him*) Mmmm. How's your mother? Coping with Christmas, is she?

WARREN: Oh, yes, she's under control.

STANLEY: Good.
(RICK *comes in with two kitchen chairs. She, too, is bright and – for her – positive.*)
Ah, Rick. A glass of sherry?

RICK: Thank you very much, Mr Inchbridge.

STANLEY: Coming up. Warren and I think it's quite a good one. We'd like your opinion.
(STANLEY *pours another glass.* RICK *sets the chairs round the table.*)
I don't know if Hazel will want one. Warren, would you mind – just asking my wife if she'd like a glass.

WARREN: Certainly, Mr Inchbridge. (*He goes out for a moment.*)

STANLEY: Where is she? I presume she intends to join us.

RICK: She was just putting things out in the kitchen. (*Taking the glass.*) Thank you.

STANLEY: Good health. Yes. Hazel's made us a little snack. For afterwards. When we've finished playing.

(WARREN *returns.*)

WARREN: She says no, thank you, she's having a fruit juice.

STANLEY: Oh, well. More for us, eh?

WARREN: She's made this big orange jelly.

STANLEY: Has she? Splendid. (*During the next, he gets out the Game board and the box of figures.*)

WARREN: And a lot of blancmange.

STANLEY: Yes, well. She always could make a fine blancmange, could Hazel.

RICK: Is that meant for us?

STANLEY: Yes. Yes, I think it probably is. Yes.

WARREN: (*Enthusiastically*) Great.

RICK: (*Less sure*) Yes.

(*Pause.*)

STANLEY: (*Casually, as he sets out the board*) So what's all your news, Rick? How's Marcie? Is she well?

RICK: She's fine.

STANLEY: Good. I haven't see her for a day or so. Give her my love, won't you?

RICK: Sure.

STANLEY: (*Slight pause*) You will remember, won't you?

RICK: Yes.

(*Pause. Along the hall, the music is switched off. Hazel's voice takes up the singing.*)

WARREN: How's Mr Skate, Mr Inchbridge? Is he any better?

STANLEY: They're keeping him in a day or two longer, Warren – thank you for asking. Giving him one or two more tests. They're pretty certain it was a mild stroke. Just a warning.

WARREN: Ah.

(HAZEL *enters. Her reversion to more youthful days continues. She has on a very short skirt, bright tights and has redone her hair in an even younger style. The effect is incongruous but not*

72

*grotesque. She has a tall glass of fruit squash, which she is
drinking through a straw. She's especially bouncy.)*

HAZEL: Sorry, folks . . . Here I am. Let's get going, I'm ready.
(She sits.)

STANLEY: *(Slightly startled)* Right. Good, well, yes, let's start.
(Indicating the lights) Warren, would you mind . . .
(The rest of them sit around the table. WARREN *does the lights.)*
Let's see what perils lie in wait for our intrepid band this
evening, eh?
(HAZEL 'gurgles' with her straw as she sucks on her drink.)
So long as we don't have a repetition of last week.

HAZEL: No way.

STANLEY: Sorry?

HAZEL: That won't happen again.

STANLEY: What makes you so sure?

HAZEL: We're the right number. Last week we had the wrong
cosmic number . . .

STANLEY: *(Doubtful)* Yes, I suppose . . .

WARREN: That's possible.

HAZEL: It's true, Dreep-droop-dee-doop-bee-barp! Brerrp!
Idonia, the Mystic, has spoken.

RICK: Hey! *(She has removed the figure of Idonia from the box and is
staring at it.)* What's happened to Idonia? What have you
done to her?

HAZEL: I just made her some new clothes . . .

WARREN: She had new clothes last week . . .

HAZEL: Well, she wanted some more. Isn't she pretty?

RICK: She looks like a fairy . . .

STANLEY: Well, I'm sure we'll all get – used to her . . . *(Looking at
the other two appealingly.)* I'm sure we will. In time. I think
she looks rather enchanting – as if she was going to a party.

HAZEL: I'm going to make her a whole wardrobe eventually.

WARREN: She's shrunk, too. Hasn't she? She's got shorter.

HAZEL: She was always small. She's the tiniest thing.

STANLEY: Shall we get on. *(Laying aside the now empty box.)* We
seem to have lost Novia altogether. Not that it matters since
Marcie's not here . . .

HAZEL: I think she fell out somewhere. In the waste disposal.

STANLEY: (*Hastily*) Right. Alric speaks to you all. Since our meeting with Balaac, we have been resting these seven days. We must assume, alas, that Novia, the Newcomer who was with us for so short a time, has been taken by him and may even now be his prisoner. Maybe our task should be to . . .
(HAZEL '*gurgles*' *her drink.*)
. . . don't do that, Hazel dear . . . should be to rescue her . . . for God help the child if she should stay for long within the clutches of Balaac. What say we?

WARREN: 'Tis a good scheme, O Wise One.

RICK: Aye.

STANLEY: Idonia child, what sayest thou?

HAZEL: (*In a slightly younger voice than before*) Sproing! I think, O Leader, bing-boing, if she be taken by Balaac she is already dead – or worse than dead. Broink! Ding! Idonia foresees this. Better we proceed with our original quest. Sprunk! Forget the silly wench.

RICK: (*Forcefully*) Nay. No way.

WARREN: Nay. We canst not do that.

STANLEY: I agree. Idonia child, you are outnumbered. The will of the majority is that we seek out Balaac and rescue her. You must obey.
(HAZEL *pouts.*)
And so we proceed. Xenon, thou of the Great Sight of the Stranger, what seest thou?

WARREN: We stand on the edge of the Dead Kingdom of Balaac to the south. Behind us to the north, the Valley of Sighs and the Mountains of Ag. To the east, the Grey River. To the west, the Kingdom of Orrich.

STANLEY: Tell us, Idonia, Enchantress, Child with the gift of Many Tongues, what seest thou?

HAZEL: (*Sulkily*) Nothing.

STANLEY: What to the north?

HAZEL: Nothing.

STANLEY: What to the south?

HAZEL: Nothing.

STANLEY: To the east?

HAZEL: Nothing.

STANLEY: Oh, come on, Hazel, for heaven's sake . . . To the west?

HAZEL: Nothing. Dwing! Nothing at all. Dwing! There is no living being in any direction, anywhere. At any time. Dwing! Idonia hath spoken. Now she is silent. Dwing! She is not going on with this quest. She thinks it's a waste of time. She is going to take the ice-cream out of the freezer.

(HAZEL *gets up and, without another word, flounces out, leaving the others still seated, speechless. As she goes,* HAZEL *flicks on the main lights. Whatever spell there was remaining is broken.* STANLEY *switches off the anglepoise.*)

STANLEY: Well . . . maybe she's right. Christmas Eve isn't perhaps the ideal time for . . . fighting the forces of . . . We will rest, friends. Idonia is right. Maybe by the time of the New Year we will be stronger. Right. Sorry. Shall we – since she's made it – perhaps we ought to go and try some of this orange jelly? Blancmange? I'll bring the sherry. We can take our glasses through . . . Perhaps you could both bring a chair – thank you . . . After you, please, lead on . . .

(STANLEY *ushers* RICK *and* WARREN *ahead of him. They both go out carrying a chair apiece plus their respective sherry glasses.* STANLEY *follows them with the tray. With a final anxious glance round the room, he switches off the light. In the kitchen,* HAZEL *is singing.*

The lights simultaneously come up on Warren't attic. The hatch opens and he squeezes through, cautiously. He shuts the hatch quietly. He crosses to his screen and turns up the volume. The single beeping sound. He fades this down. He fades up the speaker. The sound of his mother's gentle snoring. WARREN *nods. He leaves the speaker faded up. He goes and lies on the bed. He closes his eyes, concentrating deeply.*)

WARREN: Let it be soon. Let it be soon. Come to me, you beautiful Trilla! Come to me! Marcie! Marcie! Oh, Marcie! (*As he lies there,* HAZEL *comes back into the darkened sitting room.*)

HAZEL: (*Seeing the figures still lying on the table*) Tch! Tch! Tch! What are you all doing out of your box? You naughty things. (*She starts to put them away. But scarcely has she started to do so when, in her hands, the creatures appear to develop lives of their own. Thanks to accompanying dialogue from* HAZEL *— plus a little 'incidental' hummed music — the four little people contrive a daring escape off the table-top, down a table-leg and under the table.*

   Their dialogue is barely audible to anyone but HAZEL *, but if we could hear, it would probably go something like this*:)
Come on, everybody, let's get going . . . OK. Here we go, follow me. (*Tiny fanfare.*) Over the cliff, boook! Follow Herwin. Doodle-ee! Here take my hand, Idonia. Come on, Xenon, you slow-coach, don't get left behind. Peep! Help, help. I'm slipping. It's all right, I've got you. Doop! Deep! That's better. Down we go. (*A good stretch of incidental music.*) Look out. (*Dramatic chord.*) Nearly, there. Wackatow! Look, there's something following us. (*Another chord.*) Quick, under the cliff. (*Music.*) We'll be safe here. Quang! Wang! he can't see us under here.
(*A little more 'music' as* HAZEL *and the four little characters vanish under the table.* HAZEL *continues to play quietly.*

   THELMA, *via the speaker, snorts loudly in her sleep.* WARREN, *who has apparently dozed off as well, wakes with a jolt.*)
WARREN: (*With a cry*) Marcie! (*Blinking awake*) I saw her! Arnie, I saw her. She was just so beautiful . . . (*He enjoys his moment of ecstasy. Something makes him aware of his hands. He holds them up and studies them.*) My hands. What's happening to my hands? They're – they're changing. My hands are changing . . . I'm starting to change . . . (*Rising ecstatically and moving to his console.*) I must get it all finished. There's very little time. I've got very little time left . . .
(WARREN *goes to his console and works away feverishly for a moment or two. Then, during the next, he carefully opens the hatch and descends, closing it behind him.*

   STANLEY *enters the sitting room. He sees the Game board still out and starts to put it away. A tiny fanfare from under the table.* STANLEY *looks startled. He goes down on his hands and knees and sees* HAZEL.)
STANLEY: Hazel?
HAZEL: Hallo. Bloon-blip-bloon . . .
STANLEY: What are you doing? What are you doing under there, old love?

HAZEL: Playing. I'm having a play . . . Bloon!

STANLEY: Having a play?

HAZEL: With the little people.

STANLEY: With the little people? Oh, yes. Well, I think it's time for bed now, don't you, old love?

HAZEL: (*Plaintively*) I want to play . . .

STANLEY: Yes, but it's getting rather late, you see. And you've had a long day. Come on. (*He takes her hand and gently draws her out from under the table.*) That's it. Tell you what, you take those little people with you, what about that? Would you like to take them up to – to bed with you?

HAZEL: Yes. Doople-deedle . . .

STANLEY: Good. Come on, then. That's a good girl. We may have to – go out tomorrow, Hazel, to see someone . . .

HAZEL: Where are we going?

STANLEY: I'll tell you tomorrow. It's a surprise. I'll tell you tomorrow. That's it. Come on, up we go.

(*As he speaks, he gently leads* HAZEL *out of the room and upstairs to bed.*

The lights cross-fade to Rick's basement. The overhead light is on. The room is empty. There is a knock at the back door. A brief pause, then another knock. The handle is tested. The door is already unlocked. RICK *opens it and looks inside, slightly cautiously. She closes the door behind her. She stands surveying the room, very still, listening. Suddenly we hear footsteps. They are coming from the top of the stairs.* RICK *waits tense. Someone comes slowly down the stairs. We see, at length, that it is* MARCIE. *She is holding a suitcase. Her face is red and her eyes swollen from crying.*)

RICK: (*Softly*) What are you doing?

MARCIE: (*In a small, shaky voice*) I had to borrow a suitcase, I'm sorry.

RICK: Where are you going?

MARCIE: It's – it's probably best . . .

(*Further footsteps and* LARRY *is standing on the stairs above and behind* MARCIE.)

LARRY: Good evening. I dropped by to pick up my wife. I hope you've no objections. I thought it was time she got back to a normal healthy relationship. You're just in time to say goodbye.

(*He pushes* MARCIE *in front of him. She moves like a zombie.* RICK *stands motionless.* MARCIE *reaches* RICK, *who is still blocking the doorway.*)

Want to say ta-ta, then, do we? I won't look. I'll turn my back. If you'd like to give Marcie one last kiss, Alice.

RICK: (*Exploding with fury*) You bastard . . .

LARRY: (*Starting to laugh*) Now, now . . .

(*His laugh is short-lived.* RICK *delivers three or four lethal-looking martial-arts blows to Larry's body and face. The whole thing is lightning-fast.* LARRY *goes down like a dead ox. He lies unconscious.*)

MARCIE: (*In breathless admiration*) Golly!

RICK: (*Even more amazed*) It works. It actually works.

MARCIE: How is he?

RICK: He's not dead. I don't know why he isn't. Those were all supposed to be lethal blows. I obviously didn't do them quite right . . .

MARCIE: Pretty good . . .

RICK: Yes, pretty good. Hurt my hand, though . . .

MARCIE: (*Concerned*) Is it all right, let me see . . . (*She takes Rick's hand.*)

RICK: It's all right.

(LARRY *is starting to come round. He seems to be having trouble breathing through his nose. He makes a snorting noise.*)

MARCIE: He's waking up. What are we going to do . . .?

RICK: It's fine, don't worry.

MARCIE: But what if he . . . what if he . . .?

RICK: I'll hit him again, won't I?

LARRY: (*Sitting up and feeling his nose*) You broken by dose. You doe dat. You broken by bluddy dose . . . You bluddy bitch . . . Arrggh! (*He gets up, in some pain.* RICK *has probably broken his ribs as well. He dabs at his nose with an increasingly bloody handkerchief. To* MARCIE) Cub on. Are you cubbing?

MARCIE: (*Looking at them both in turn*) No.

LARRY: You cub or I'll break your deck, you liddle brick deaser. (*He lurches forward.*)

RICK: You lay one finger on her and I promise you, you'll never walk again. I'll break both your legs.
    (LARRY *hesitates*.)
    Come on. Want to try it? Come on.
    (*A moment*. LARRY *retreats to the door*.)
LARRY: I'll be back – donchoo worry . . .
RICK: I wouldn't advise it . . . Goodbye. Off you go.
    (LARRY *opens the outside door and steps out*.)
LARRY: (*Just before he leaves*) You broken by dose, you doe. Bluddy desbian dyke bitches . . .
    (LARRY *goes, closing the door behind him*. MARCIE *immediately moves and locks it*.)
MARCIE: Are you all right?
RICK: (*Shrugging nonchalantly*) Yes, yes . . .
MARCIE: You were fantastic.
RICK: Well . . .
MARCIE: Do you want anything . . . Tea or . . .
RICK: No. I'm OK.
    (*She sits*. MARCIE *moves to her*.)
MARCIE: I didn't – I wasn't . . . I was only leaving because – because he threatened to hurt you if I didn't. I mean, that was the only reason. I didn't want to go with him.
RICK: Whatever. (*Shrugs again*.)
MARIE: (*Smiling*) And I promise you, I never told him about your name. I promise. He saw the note up there. You do believe that, don't you?
RICK: Yes. I believe you. Why shouldn't I?
    (MARCIE *sits by her and takes her hand*.)
MARCIE: We ought to burn it. Before anyone else reads it. We ought to burn everything up there. Start again. What do you say?
    (RICK *snatches her hand away and rises*.)
    Sorry, did I hurt your hand?
RICK: No.
MARCIE: You don't like – people touching you very much, do you?
RICK: I don't mind. Why?
MARCIE: I just wondered.
    (*A silence*.)

79

RICK: (*Softly*) He used to . . . him . . . the man my mother lived
with . . . upstairs . . . he used to . . . try and touch me.
Sometimes. I wasn't that young. I was fourteen. Or fifteen.
(*A pause.* MARCIE *waits.*)
Don't tell your mum. Just our secret, Alice. Don't tell your
mum. Come on, Alice. There's a good girl. Isn't that nice,
Alice? Doesn't that feel good? . . . One day he hurt me and I
kicked him. And he hit me. And my mum saw the bruise.
And she asked me how I got it. So I told her.
(*Pause.*)
But she didn't believe me. She couldn't believe me, could
she? If she believed me, what would that make him? And if
he was that, what would that do to her, who couldn't live
without him? So he lied – of course – and she believed him.
Because that was how she wanted it to be.
(*Pause.*)
He stayed Mr Wonderful, so what did that make me, eh? A
jealous little teenage tart who tried to screw her mother's
boyfriend. So she took him away. Away from temptation.
Away from me.
(*Pause.*)
I don't like people touching me very much, no.
(MARCIE *stands looking at her. She is very moved, but unsure
what to do for the best.* RICK *looks at her, eventually. She is
propped against the table, half sitting, half standing.* MARCIE
smiles weakly. RICK *holds out a hand, rather awkwardly.*
MARCIE *moves and takes it. They stand.* MARCIE *kisses her
lightly on the mouth.* RICK *responds. They smile at each other.*)
MARCIE: (*Suddenly a little awkward, glances at her watch*) It's
Christmas Day, you know. Happy Christmas.
RICK: (*Pulling away*) Just a second . . .
MARCIE: (*Smiling*) Where are you going now?
RICK: Wait. (*She rummages in her bag and produces a small parcel
inexpertly wrapped. She holds it out to* MARCIE *rather self-
consciously.*) Here you are. Happy Christmas.
MARCIE: Thank you. (*She takes it.*) We should wait till the
morning really.
RICK: Doesn't matter.

MARCIE: Well, OK. (*She opens the parcel.*) What have I got? What have I got? What's this? (*She has torn away the wrapping to reveal a small jeweller's box.*) Hey! What has she bought me in this lovely little – (*She breaks off as she sees the contents.*) Oh.

RICK: (*Anxiously*) Is it all right?

MARCIE: (*A bit stunned*) It's just beautiful. It's lovely. It's gorgeous. (*She takes a small antique pendant out of the box and holds it up.*) It's the most beautiful thing I've ever seen. Thank you. Where did you – ? No, I mustn't ask that.

RICK: It was mine. I got given it. By some old aunt. I never wore it.

MARCIE: But don't you want to keep it?

RICK: I don't wear pendants much. I look a bit stupid. Get caught up in the handlebars.

MARCIE: Well, I'll certainly wear it. (*Kissing her*) Thank you. I must try it on . . . No, wait, wait a minute. (*She puts the pendant on the table.*) You can have just one of yours now. Just one. You can't have the others till tomorrow morning . . . (*As she speaks,* MARCIE *has darted off momentarily. She now returns with a splendidly wrapped fair-sized parcel.*) Here you are. I can't even remember what this one is. I certainly haven't got you anything as splendid as that. Here.

RICK: Thank you. (*She starts to open it.*)

MARCIE: Read the card. Read the card first.

RICK: Oh, yes. (*She does so.*) Oh, yes. Thank you.

MARCIE: I mean it. Every word.

RICK: (*Slightly embarrassed again*) Thank you. (*She removes the wrapping paper to reveal a cardboard box.*)

MARCIE: (*Giggling delightedly*) Oh, I know what this is. It's this. This is for both of us really.

RICK: I don't know what this can be. (*She opens the box and takes out a cooking utensil. She stares at it.*)

MARCIE: It's an omelette pan. Do you like it?

RICK: (*Smiling bravely through her disappointment*) It's great. It's really good.

MARCIE: It's what we needed, isn't it?

RICK: We did. Amazing. (*She waves it vaguely.*) Heavy.

MARCIE: They need to be heavy. It's a good one. Made in France.

I'm going to try on my lovely pendant. (*She grabs the pendant and hurries off.*) See what it looks like . . .

(RICK *stands rather crestfallen with her omelette pan. Then starts to follow* MARCIE *off.* MARCIE, *delighted cry, off.*)

Oh, it's gorgeous. It's going to go with practically everything I have.

RICK: (*To herself*) Good. (*A look at the pan, ruefully*) So will this.

(RICK *goes off as the lights cross-fade to Warren's attic.*

WARREN *is emerging through the hatch. He has on dark glasses. He leaves the hatch open and sits at his console. He has an air of a man dealing with an imminent emergency. He presses down his mike switch and speaks.*)

WARREN: (*His voice booming down the stairs through numerous speakers*) Mother . . . Mother . . . Are you awake?

(*He presses another switch. We hear Thelma's startled voice from a loudspeaker on the wall.*)

THELMA: (*Her voice, waking with a start*) Warren . . . what's happening? It's half-past five.

WARREN: Mother, this is your son Warren speaking. I must ask you for the next few hours not to leave your room unless you are given clearance by me to do so.

THELMA: What are you talking about? It's Christmas morning, Warren . . .

WARREN: I'm sorry, Mother . . .

THELMA: I have to cook your dinner . . .

WARREN: There will be no dinner today, Mother, I'm sorry. I am having to switch on the force fields to prevent unauthorized movement around the house . . .

THELMA: Warren, I can't stop in here all day. I have to go to Mass.

WARREN: (*Pressing down a switch*) Mother, there is now mains voltage running through your bedroom door handle.

THELMA: Warren, son. Let me try and get Father Kennedy round to see you, would that help . . .?

WARREN: Please remain where you are. I will be monitoring your movements at all time.

THELMA: Warren, please, he'd know what to do for the best, you see. You might need an exorcism . . .

WARREN: That is all, Mother. (*He cuts off both the speaker and the mike. He rises and looks at himself in the mirror. Touching his face*) It's happening. It's happening all over me.
(*He hurries for the hatchway and scrambles off down the ladder. As he does this, the lights come up on the Inchbridges' sitting room.*

STANLEY *is leading* MARCIE *into the room. He has the look of a man who wasn't expecting company. He is in his dressing gown. He seems a little tireder, even older than before.* MARCIE *is as spruce and trim as ever. She carries a bag filled with Christmas parcels. She is wearing her new pendant.*)

MARCIE: (*As they enter*) I hope you don't object to people coming round on Christmas Morning?

STANLEY: No, no. It's splendid to see you. It's a lovely surprise . . .

MARCIE: I don't know, at home we just had this tradition –

STANLEY: Fine. Please. Sit down.

MARCIE: Just literally for a second. I've got one or two more people to see. Left Rick fast asleep. She can sleep round the clock if you let her . . . Now . . . (*She examines her carrier.*) Oh, yes. That's Warren's. Called round there just now. I couldn't get a reply. Maybe he and his mother have gone away.

STANLEY: (*Doubtful*) Possibly.

MARCIE: (*Finding her three gifts*) Here we are. Just little things.

STANLEY: (*Concealing a yawn*) Thank you.

MARCIE: I didn't wake you up, did I?

STANLEY: No, no. I've been up for hours. Hazel tends to wake very early these days.

MARCIE: How is she?

STANLEY: Oh, fine. Splendid. She's around – somewhere.

MARCIE: She was looking terrific the last time I saw her . . . Look, this is for her. It's just a sort of embroidery kit . . . I know she likes sewing and making things . . . It might not be her sort of thing at all but –

STANLEY: Lovely. It could just be a trifle – complicated – for her –

MARCIE: Oh, I shouldn't think so . . .

83

STANLEY: It has sharp needles and things, does it?

MARCIE: Oh, yes . . .

STANLEY: Well, we'll see. (*Laying the present aside and turning to another smaller parcel.*) What's this?

MARCIE: Oh, that's a book for Mr Skate. It's a dictionary. Just a baby one, I know he's fond of words.

STANLEY: Oh, yes, that's splendid. I'll make sure he gets it.

MARCIE: Will he be coming home soon?

STANLEY: Er – probably not for some little while yet. He's a lot better. He's recovered well from the second stroke. He's not yet regained his speech but he's sitting up and taking notice.

MARCIE: Good. Give him my best wishes.

STANLEY: I will. (*He picks up the third parcel.*)

MARCIE: That's for you. Now that's really, really, really silly. I just couldn't resist it.

STANLEY: What on earth is this?

(*The package reveals a small, inexpensive, unexceptional if quite appealing china or plaster dog.* STANLEY, *literally lost for words.*)

Good heavens.

MARCIE: Isn't he sweet? I just fell in love with him. I had to buy him for someone and I thought of you. I thought he could be in your game. A talking dog. Have you ever had a talking dog?

STANLEY: No . . .

MARCIE: You should.

STANLEY: He's splendid. What a – splendid face. As a matter of fact, I – well, I wasn't expecting to see you today so I haven't even wrapped it properly – just a minute . . . (STANLEY *rises and goes to the sideboard. He rummages in a drawer, searching for his gift. Finding a small brown paper bag.*) Yes, here we are. Not very elegantly wrapped but – here we are, anyway. Forgive the wrapping paper.

(MARCIE *takes her present from the bag. It is another pendant. A modern one with nowhere near the value or the style of the one she is wearing.*)

MARCIE: Oh, you shouldn't have given me this.

STANLEY: Do you like it?

MARCIE: It must have been terribly expensive

STANLEY: I noticed you wore things like that sometimes.

MARCIE: Yes, I do. All the time. Look. (*She displays the one she is wearing.*)

STANLEY: Oh, yes. That's really nice. Nicer than that one.

MARCIE: (*Tactfully*) No. They're just – different. Thank you.
(*She bends forward to kiss him on the cheek. He tries to kiss her on the lips. It is a very clumsy exchange. They both step back in slight embarrassment.*
As they do this, HAZEL *enters the room. She is crawling on her hands and knees and pushing a toy vehicle of some description.*
MARCIE *stares at her in natural surprise.* STANLEY *seems barely to notice her.*)

HAZEL: (*Making her car sounds*) . . . brrrmmm! Brrrmmm! Brrrmmm! . . .

MARCIE: (*Staring in horror at* HAZEL) Is she all right? Mrs Inchbridge? Is anything wrong?

STANLEY: No. She plays like that for hours. (*Speaking loudly.*) Hazel! Hazel, darling! (*Indicating the vehicle.*) Her Christmas present. Look who's here. Hazel!
(HAZEL *looks up somewhat myopically.*)
Hazel, do you know who this is? It's Marcie. Say hallo. Hallo, Marcie.

HAZEL: Hallo-mercy . . . Bloop! Blooooop!

MARCIE: Hallo, Mrs . . . Hazel. (*Lost for words.*) She's – she's –

STANLEY: (*Picking up the toy dog*) Hazel, what's this? What's this then? What's this? Do you know what this is?
(HAZEL *extends both her hands to show she wants it.*)
Yes. You tell me what it is first.

HAZEL: Bow-wow.

STANLEY: Good. There you are. (*He gives it to her.*) What do you say?

HAZEL: 'kyou.

STANLEY: Thank you. You play with that. And don't put it in your mouth. (*To* MARCIE) She puts everything in her mouth. She's a terror.

HAZEL: (*Playing*) . . . brrrmm. Wooof! Woof! Brrmm!

STANLEY: Quietly, Hazel. We're trying to talk.

(HAZEL *crawls under the table*.)

That's it. You go under there then.

(*As* HAZEL *disappears*, STANLEY *reaches down to feel her rather bulky backside. Apologetically*.)

Make sure she's dry. She gets a bit damp mid-mornings.

HAZEL: (*From under the table*) Beep-beep . . .

MARCIE: Stanley, what's the matter with Hazel exactly? What's happened to her . . .?

STANLEY: (*Impetuously*) Let's talk about us for a minute, could we, please? I want to talk about us.

MARCIE: Us?

STANLEY: Hazel's fine. It's us. You and me. That's what we need to talk about.

MARCIE: What about?

(*At this point*, HAZEL *pushes her vehicle along the ground to* STANLEY, *who even as he talks bends and absently pushes it back to her. Promptly*, HAZEL *pushes the vehicle back again, this time to* MARCIE, *who similarly crouches and pushes it back to* HAZEL *whilst still trying to listen to* STANLEY. *Gradually, whilst* STANLEY *is still speaking, the three engage in a vehicle exchange, crouching on the floor and pushing the toy from one to the other*. HAZEL *enjoys this no end*. MARCIE *tries to concentrate on both at once*. STANLEY *blurts out his feelings, almost oblivious to what is happening*.)

STANLEY: Our – love. My love for you. And – so I hope – your love for me. I mean – there's no point in trying to pretend otherwise – things have not been right between Hazel and I – Hazel and me – for years. In fact, if you want the truth, I don't think they've ever been right. Not since the day we married. Now, I think I could have put up with it, I think I could, I think I could have seen it through till death us do part. Only one day I meet someone like you – and I'm suddenly offered the chance of escape, the chance to do things I've never had a chance to do before. To give something to someone for a change, something that I know they need from me, would be willing to accept from me. Because unless you meet someone in this life who's prepared to take things from you, how can you decently hope to take

86

things from them in return. And if you're unable to do either of those things, what chance have you ever got of finding happiness? Do you see what I'm saying?
(*The game stops abruptly. Silence.*)

MARCIE: I don't actually know what you're talking about.

STANLEY: I'm talking about you and me, Marcie. Starting again together somewhere. A new life.

MARCIE: Living together?

STANLEY: Yes.

MARCIE: Me and you?

STANLEY: Yes.

(*A silence.* HAZEL *bangs the table-leg.*)
Hazel, don't do that, darling. (*To* MARCIE) What do you say? Say yes.

MARCIE: I – I don't know what to say. I had no idea you . . . I never thought for a minute you . . . I'm – I don't know what to say. It wouldn't work. It's impossible.

STANLEY: (*Stunned*) Impossible? Why? Why?

MARCIE: Well, we're – just not right, are we . . .? I'm – I mean, I'm – oh, golly, this is difficult to say – I don't want to hurt your feelings but – you're – well, you're old. I mean, much older than me. Aren't you?

STANLEY: A little. Not that much.

MARCIE: No, much. Much, much. Really. It wouldn't work – even if – I felt anything – like – which I don't.

STANLEY: These things have worked before . . .

MARCIE: Oh, yes. But that's only old men wanting a bit of the other before they drop dead, isn't it?

STANLEY: I'm not like that. I'm not an old man after a bit of the other . . .

MARCIE: I know you're not. That's what I'm saying. You'd want us for life, wouldn't you?

STANLEY: Of course.

MARCIE: Well, what about me? By the time I'm at an age where I could really do with someone, someone to look after me, you'd be dead. I mean, that's terribly cruel. But it's true. Isn't it?

STANLEY: (*Crushed*) How old do you think I am? I'm not that old.

MARCIE: (*Kindly*) No, but you will be, Stanley, don't you see? Much sooner than I will.

(*Silence.*)

I'd better go.

(*She rises.* STANLEY *remains seated. In a daze.*)

Thank you very, very much for asking me. I'm terribly flattered. (*She picks up her carrier and moves to the door. She leaves her locket on the table. Stooping to look under the table.*) Goodbye, Hazel. Happy Christmas.

HAZEL: Happy Mistmas – Hismas – Kissmas . . .

MARCIE: (*Just as she is going*) Stanley – you are going to – let someone – have a look at Hazel, aren't you? Examine her. I mean, she needs help, doesn't she? There's something very wrong. Don't you think so?

STANLEY: (*Wearily*) God knows. I don't know. All I know is she's happy, Marcie. She's happier than she's ever been in her whole life. Can that be wrong?

MARCIE: Well. Yes. I still think she should see someone. I really do. Still, it's up to you. She's your wife. Bye.

STANLEY: (*Sadly*) Bye.

(MARCIE *goes.* HAZEL *sings and chortles and mutters under the table.* STANLEY *rises to the window to watch* MARCIE *leave. As he stands there, Hazel's little fist comes from under the table. She grabs the end of the locket chain that* MARCIE *has left dangling over the edge. She pulls it off. The sound causes* STANLEY *to turn.*)

Hazel, what are you doing? What have you got now?

(HAZEL *has put the locket in her mouth.*)

Hazel, take that out of your mouth at once. Come on. Come on. Or else I'll get cross.

(STANLEY *bends under the table and prises the locket from Hazel's jaws.*)

That's it. That's better, thank you. Not lockets. Mustn't eat lockets. Not for mouths . . . Aaarrgg! (*He straightens up and his back gives.*) Oh, oh. That's agony. Come on, Hazel, in the kitchen. Ow! Ow! Ow! Come on.

(*He is in some pain.* HAZEL *has come out from under the table. She holds up her arms to be carried.*)

88

No, darling, I can't carry you. You're much too heavy, you see? Why do you think my back's hurting? You'll have to crawl, come on. I'll give you a biscuit. Come on, in the kitchen.

(*He stops in the doorway to let her crawl ahead of him. As she passes, he pushes her bottom to encourage her on her way.*
STANLEY *irritably, wiping his hand on his dressing gown*)

Oh, Hazel, don't tell me you need changing as well . . .

(STANLEY *limps off.* WARREN *appears crawling up the ladder. He is breathing heavily – he appears to be running some sort of fever. He presses the mike and speaker switches.*)

WARREN: (*Speaking with difficulty*) Mother, hold on. It won't be for much longer, I promise you.

THELMA: (*From the speaker*) I'm praying for you, son. I'm praying for you. Would you like a nice hot cup of tea?

WARREN: Please, Mother. Later, later. I'm tired. I'm going to have to save my strength.

(*He switches off the speaker and the mike. He half crawls to the bed. He leans against it, huddled on the floor, shivering, half in a sort of feverish trance.*

Lights up in the basement. It is daytime. RICK *comes downstairs from the house. She is in her work clothes and very dirty and tired. She is lugging two huge plastic sacks of rubbish. She drags them to the back door.*)

MARCIE: (*Calling from upstairs*) Darling!

RICK: (*Yelling*) Hallo!

MARCIE: When you come up can you bring the vacuum cleaner?

RICK: (*Yelling*) OK. (*She starts to lug the sacks out into the area outside. To herself.*) Oh, my God. What have we started? (MARCIE *appears on the stairs. She has on her headscarf and heavy-duty rubber gloves.*)

MARCIE: Darling! Rick!

RICK: (*Reappearing*) Yeah.

MARCIE: You managing all right?

RICK: Yes, I'm OK.

MARCIE: Don't overtire yourself, darling. Rest if you need to.

RICK: (*Plodding towards the kitchen*) I will.

MARCIE: Bad news. I'm afraid there's three more bags up here.

RICK: (*Going off*) Yes, OK.

MARCIE: There's mountains to get rid of. We may need to get a skip eventually, if they won't take it away.

(MARCIE *goes off upstairs.* RICK *reappears with the (new) vacuum cleaner. She heads for the stairs.* MARCIE *off, upstairs.*)

Rick! Rick, darling.

RICK: Hallo.

MARCIE: (*Off*) Do you feel strong enough to move the sideboard now, please?

RICK: Yes, yes, yes . . .

MARCIE: (*Off*) Sorry, darling . . .

(*She limps off wearily.*

The lights fade on the basement. In the attic, the computer suddenly sets off several alarms at once. WARREN *comes out of his daze. He leaps up and kills the alarms. As he does so he becomes aware of his 'new' self.*)

WARREN: (*Incredulously*) It's happened. It's worked. It's worked. (*He looks in the mirror.*) My God, look at me. Look at me. (*He laughs with joy.*) I'm a Lak! I'm a Lak! I'm a full-grown Lak! Marcie! Look at me now, Marcie! (*Remembering.*) Mother . . . Mother!

(*He goes to the console and presses both the mike and the speaker keys. There is a low indistinct moaning from the speaker. The sound of* THELMA *recovering.*)

Mother! Mother!

THELMA: (*Weakly, from the speaker*) Warren? Is that you?

WARREN: Are you all right . . .?

THELMA: I tried to open the door. I was thrown across the room . . .

WARREN: Mother, I told you to stay where you were . . .

THELMA: I needed the toilet, Warren. I've been waiting ages. Are you all right, son? How are you? I thought you'd died.

WARREN: I'm fine, Mother, Happy Christmas. And God bless us every one.

THELMA: Warren, it's Boxing Day.

WARREN: Is it? (*Startled.*) Is it? (*He starts to switch things off.*) Mother, I'm switching everything off now. You can come out.

THELMA: Oh, thank heavens . . .

WARREN: Mother . . .

THELMA: Yes.

WARREN: Make us both a cup of tea.

THELMA: (*Radiantly*) Oh, I will. I will, son. As soon as I've . . . I'll bring it up to you.

WARREN: No, you won't. I'll come down and have it with you. We'll have tea together, Mother. What about that?

THELMA: (*Ecstatically*) Oh, dear God! It's a miracle.

(WARREN *switches off the mike and the speaker. He laughs excitedly. He has another look in the mirror at himself.*)

WARREN: (*Joyously*) Marcie . . . Look at me now, Marcie. Can you see me? It's the real me! (*His laughter slowly dies. A thought has occurred. In growing alarm.*) What if she can't see me? What if she can't see me . . .?

(*With this sobering thought he starts to descend the ladder.*

In the Inchbridges' sitting room it is now evening. The lights are on.

RICK *carries through the two kitchen chairs. Her image has altered somewhat — presumably Marcie's influence. Instead of the anonymous, classless uniform, she is now off-the-peg slightly trendy. No danger of a dress but a sharp, slightly 'macho' outfit, perhaps in leather.*

STANLEY *follows her in with the anglepoise. He has a walking stick and appears to be moving with some difficulty. He's still in his dressing gown. He seems older and greyer altogether.*)

STANLEY: (*As they enter*) Thanks so much . . . I'm sorry I'm absolutely useless at the moment . . .

RICK: Can you manage?

STANLEY: Yes, it's this – bloody back – pardon the language. It's a trapped nerve, they think. Which makes it impossible to do practically anything. Can't even dress myself . . .

RICK: (*Taking the anglepoise*) I'll do that.

STANLEY: Thank you. (*He sits.*) You're looking good, if you don't mind my saying so.

RICK: (*Unused to compliments*) Oh, yes.

STANLEY: Nice hair. And – er the . . . (*He indicates her outfit.*)

RICK: Oh. Yes. I got it in the sale. Marcie persuaded me to buy it.

STANLEY: (*Dully*) How is Marcie?

RICK: (*Evasively*) Fine, she's – fine.

STANLEY: Good.

RICK: She said she might look in later.

STANLEY: Ah. Good.

> (WARREN *enters carrying* HAZEL. *She is curled up like a baby. She is very sleepy and looks fresh from her bath. Her hair is soft and fluffy, her face pink and contented.* WARREN *is barely recognizable. He has on thick green gauntlets and a green ski mask. No portion of him is actually visible.* RICK, *meanwhile, has got out the board and the four figures. It will be noticeable – if it wasn't already – that the four now resemble their playing images quite closely.*)

WARREN: My, you're a heavy girl, aren't you?

HAZEL: (*Singing happily*) Doo-boo-boo-boo . . .

STANLEY: Thank you, Warren. She doesn't need to be carried, she can walk perfectly well. Can't you, you naughty girl . . .? Put her in the chair there, Warren, put her in the chair. She can sit up on her own, she's a big girl.

> (WARREN *does this. He is very good with* HAZEL.)

WARREN: She is. There you are. You sit there. What do you say?

HAZEL: 'kyou.

WARREN: Thank you, that's right. Well done. Don't suck your thumb or it'll fall off, won't it? Shall I do the lights, Mr Inchbridge?

STANLEY: Would you, Warren? Thank you.

> (WARREN *switches off the overheads. They gather round the table.*)

It's just a skin condition you've got, is it, Warren?

WARREN: Yes, that sort of thing, Mr Inchbridge.

STANLEY: Are you seeing someone about it?

WARREN: Well, apparently it'll just be a matter of time. I have to keep it covered up, though.

RICK: Permanently?

WARREN: Yes. At present.

STANLEY: Awkward.

WARREN: I get a few looks from people.

STANLEY: You would. All right, we'd better get it over with, I suppose. This is a sad occasion, really – after all these years, but –

(HAZEL *has started banging the table.*)

Don't do that, Hazel . . . Warren, give her Idonia to play with, would you?

WARREN: (*Doing so*) There you are.

HAZEL: (*Delighted*) Idonia . . .

WARREN: Yes, you play with that.

HAZEL: Idonia . . .

STANLEY: Friends, we all know why we're here. The Game – this Game that's given us so much pleasure and excitement for – five years? – more than that – hath – has finally run its course. As I think was clearly demonstrated when we last met – the board is now empty for us – Balaac is finally dead. Our quest is over and Idonia, Xenon, Herwin, Alric must go back in their box for ever . . .

(HAZEL *is banging again.*)

Hazel, don't do that or I'll have to put you to bed.

WARREN: I'll take her, Mr Inchbridge, I'll take her . . .

STANLEY: Thank you, Warren, that's very kind.

(WARREN *takes* HAZEL *on to his knee. She croons softly.*)

There, Hazel, aren't you lucky? You're a spoilt girl, aren't you? So are we agreed, friends, the Game is concluded?

RICK: (*Sadly*) Agreed.

WARREN: (*Gloomily*) Agreed. (*Gently.*) You agree, don't you, Hazel?

HAZEL: (*In a tiny sleepy voice*) Yeth.

WARREN: She agrees.

STANLEY: Well, that's it. I thought perhaps we might all take our own figures away with us. As a memento. Would that be a nice idea? Yes.

(*They all pick up their pieces.* HAZEL *still clutches hers.*)

So.

None of them feels like moving. They all sit and stare at the board rather sadly. Suddenly, the overhead lights flood on. They all jump. It is MARCIE.)

MARCIE: Hey, sorry – it's only me. It was so quiet in here I thought you'd all . . . The door was open. You all OK?

STANLEY: Yes.

RICK: Yes.

WARREN: Fine.

MARCIE: Who's that? Is that Warren?

WARREN: Yes.

MARCIE: Why are you like that?

STANLEY: He has a skin condition.

MARCIE: What sort of skin condition?

WARREN: One all over my skin . . .

MARCIE: Let's have a look . . .

WARREN: No, no, it's OK.

RICK: (*Feebly*) Leave him . . .

MARCIE: Have you been to see anyone about it?

WARREN: No, no, honestly . . . it's . . .

MARCIE: Well, you should. (*Firmly*.) Warren! Let me have a look. Come on! Let me see, at once! Put her down. And take that thing off.

(WARREN *puts* HAZEL *back in her chair*.)

Come on! Come into the light.

(WARREN *moves to her.* MARCIE *waits. Slowly he takes off his gloves, then his mask. His face, of course, is perfectly normal.* MARCIE *tilts his face and examines it sternly and critically like a fierce nurse*.)

WARREN: (*Anxiously*) Can you see anything?

MARCIE: Nothing. You look just the same as usual to me. You stupid thing. It's all in your head. (*To* RICK) Darling, I'm leaving the shopping with you, all right? Can you bring it home on the bike?

RICK: Yes.

MARCIE: Don't be too late, will you?

RICK: No.

MARCIE: 'night, all. 'night, Stanley. 'night, 'night, Hazel.

(HAZEL *blows a raspberry*.)

Oh, that's not a very nice thing to do, Hazel, is it? Naughty girl. I'll switch this out again, shall I? 'night.

(MARCIE *switches off the overheads and goes. Silence.* HAZEL *has still been clutching Idonia in her hand. She clumps it down suddenly on the board. The other three stare. Then, as if by silent*

agreement, *in turn,* RICK *replaces Herwin on the board;*
WARREN *replaces Xenon;* STANLEY *finally replaces Alric.*)
STANLEY: (*Softly*) Onwards?
WARREN: Onwards.
RICK: Onwards.
HAZEL: (*With a childish giggle*) Onwards!
  (*Blackout.*)